HISTORY THE TEACHER

D1784700

HISTORY THE TEACHER
Education Inspired by Humanity's Story

FREDERICK J. GOULD

Volume 98

Routledge
Taylor & Francis Group

LONDON AND NEW YORK

First published in 1921

This edition first published in 2012
by Routledge
2 Park Square, Milton Park, Abingdon, Oxfordshire OX14 4RN

Simultaneously published in the USA and Canada
by Routledge
711 Third Avenue, New York, NY 10017

First issued in paperback 2014

Routledge is an imprint of the Taylor and Francis Group, an informa company

© 1921 Frederick J. Gould

British Library Cataloguing in Publication Data
A catalogue record for this book is available from the British Library

ISBN 13: 978-0-415-68939-7 (Volume 98)
ISBN 13: 978-0-415-75087-5 (pbk)

Publisher's Note
The publisher has gone to great lengths to ensure the quality of this reprint but points out that some imperfections in the original copies may be apparent.

Disclaimer
The publisher has made every effort to trace copyright holders and would welcome correspondence from those they have been unable to trace.

HISTORY
THE TEACHER

EDUCATION INSPIRED
BY HUMANITY'S STORY

BY

FREDERICK J. GOULD

WITH A PREFACE BY
F. W. SANDERSON, M.A.

METHUEN & CO. LTD.
36 ESSEX STREET W.C.
LONDON

First Published in 1921

CONTENTS

CHAPTER   PAGE

PREFACE - - - - - vii

I. HISTORY THE SUPREME THEME - - 3

II. THE EARLY AGE - - - - 27

III. THE CATHOLIC-FEUDAL AGE - - 59

IV. THE AGE OF EXPANSION - - - 83

V. THE SCHEME RENEWED FOR ADOLESCENTS - 117

INDEX - - - - - 131

TABLES

HISTORY OF HUMANITY (FOR AGES 6—14) - - 2

,,   ,,   (FOR ADOLESCENTS) - 116

,,   ,,   (ADAPTED TO INDIA) - 129

PREFACE

I HAVE gladly responded to the request to write a foreword to Mr. Gould's book. The book comes to me as a great inspiration. Mr. Gould's school is not simply a place where boys undergo the operation of having their faculties sharpened ; it is not entirely filled with tool-sharpening class-rooms ; it is a home or workshop for creative life. One single purpose pervades the life of the school, and through this purpose the life and work are directed and controlled. The purpose is the cause of humanity, the service of the community. The author is possessed with this idea, and to it all the methods of the school, the " studies," the organization, are made to bend. He pictures a head master commissioned to the service of man, and sees him directing all the activities, and capacities, and tendencies of the school to this one end, bending all these gifts to the common service. Such is the spirit which seems to me to pervade the book, and all its multiplicities of catalogues, and charts, and instructions.

And there is no doubt that a school can be engaged in a community service. A school can be organized

as a body of workers, researching, investigating, dis-
covering, appreciating, making ; in units or in groups
as is needed, with definite constructive work all concerned with the welfare and wants of man to-day.
Such service will lead to a new and a greater sacrifice,
to a deeper and more effective quality of love, of mercy,
of justice, of service, a fuller social service.

Mr. Gould formulates a body of method for the aim
he has in view. His method takes the form of history.
He sets out to show how man can be raised by studying
how man has been raised in the past ages. His book
presents a live museum and library, full of all sorts of
material needed for the investigation and appreciation
of man's history. At first sight the apparent medley
of things seems bewildering ; but it will begin to take
up a shape or form, and will impress the workers with
the beauty and power of abundance. Here is a well-
equipped and inspired guide so that anyone can read.
The whole is organized and arranged as an " index "
to the life of man, and grows into an objective guide to
humanity's story. There is plentiful material for
research, for delving ; the facts of life can be readjusted ;
fresh judgments can be formed and new values made.
Wandering about in these spacious homes or gardens,
the whole school can be a kind of Psyche's task, re-
sorting the boxing of right and wrong, of good and evil.
It is the material for history in a wide sense, for the
crafts are there, and science ; but Mr. Gould has not
undertaken the other essential element in the life
of man—the work of science in workshop and laboratory.

A splendid guide it is to a wealth of knowledge, to
great homes of knowledge. To possess such abundance

is the true need of the time—a need which any community could satisfy if it would. But Mr. Gould is
driven by the veritable poverty of our educational
system to do the best he can by placing most of the
teaching in the hands of masters. It is pathetic, but
so it is. The library is not there, the museum is not
there. Mr. Gould tells the teacher how he can do
without them. Want of material (poverty) throws the
author on to the inspiration of the teaching, and his
pupils learn to be receptive, but not so creative. The
fault lies with those who hold the finance. In other
hands Mr. Gould's " library " and " museum " might
degenerate into methods dictated by poverty. Poverty
shows its influence in all kinds of methods and values.
It has exaggerated the belief in the stimulus of pleasure,
of beauty, of play, of so-called interest ; but the fuller
and truer stimulus for boys and girls of all ages will be
found in the bountiful opportunity of working for the
community, and the study of the " interesting," the
" inspiring," will not be necessary.

Mr. Gould has sought to reach his objective through
history ; but scientific readers will know that history
is only half the life of man. History cannot be divorced
from science and the crafts, nor can science and the
crafts be divorced from history. In this book the
author's concern with science and the crafts is in their
effect on the life of man—he is not here concerned with
how they create and change the standards of value ;
but the root of the matter is there, and we can heartily
join with him in all that he says regarding it.

Education inspired by humanity's story must be
supplemented, perhaps created, by education inspired
by humanity's needs. The ideal school should have

two groups of buildings—the library-museum block ;
the science laboratory, gardens, fields, workshops ; and
rising up between them should be the temple of man's
making and his doing.

For the first of these groups the book here given is
an enthusiastic specification and guide.

F. W. SANDERSON

THE SCHOOL, OUNDLE,
    21 *March,* 1921

HISTORY THE TEACHER

TABLE OF WORLD HISTORY

TIME BEFORE MAN (*many millions of years*).	Nebula, or fire-mist. (?) Sun and planets. Earth, its sponges, corals, shell-fish, sea-weeds; granite. Fish, insects, reptiles, birds; moss, trees, flowers; slate, sandstone, coal, limestone, chalk. Mammals; monkey-like or ape-like men, 500,000 or more years ago. Ice age.

HISTORY OF HUMANITY

EARLY AGE *to about* A.D. 400.	Primitive man. Growth of villages, cities, nations. Slavery. Egypt, Babylon, Greece, Rome, India, China. Jews and their neighbour-nations. Christians and Early Church.
CATHOLIC-FEUDAL AGE *to about* 1300.	Church, popes, monks, nuns. Arabia and Mohammedans. Barons and serfs. Towns and guilds. Parliaments. Universities. Use of money extended.
AGE OF EXPANSION (of learning, science, art, trade, nationality, democracy, and of mankind over the globe) *to the War*, 1914–1918, *and the League of Nations*, 1919.	Printing-press; spread of learning. Routes to India and America; circumnavigation of globe; trading companies. Protestants, Puritans. English revolution. Beginnings of British Empire-Commonwealth, and of N. and S. American Colonies. Spread of machinery. American and French Revolutions. Australasia colonized. South American Republics. Negro-slavery abolished. Trade Unionists and Co-operators. Suffrage, popular education, sanitation. German Empire. Italian unity. Rise of Japan. African Colonies. Socialists. Union of S. Africa, completing the Home-rule series, Canada, Newfoundland, Australia, New Zealand, S. Africa. World practically explored and mapped. British Commonwealth renewed in war, and its friendships with U.S., France, Italy, etc., strengthened.

HISTORY THE TEACHER

CHAPTER I

HISTORY THE SUPREME THEME

THE aim of education should be service of family and commonwealth, expressed in material, intellectual, and artistic industry, inspired by history, and perpetually responsive to the claims of the whole circle of humanity ; and this duty of service applies to all members of the community, without exception.

By " history " as treated in the present study, is meant the story, or tale, or " spell " of human love,[1] human order (material, moral, æsthetic, intellectual, social) and human progress, or evolution, realized in individual lives and in the life of communities ; the story unfolding from the pre-human times, when the earth gradually prepared itself as man's habitation, down to the present moment, and the present step into the future. Whatever can be recorded in a " spell," in speech or writing, is history, whether it relates to the happenings of a

---

[1] " Gospel," originally meaning " good spell," came also, in certain Northern languages, to mean " God-spell," or God-history. The Bible was written and compiled essentially as a history book ; its Genesis describing primitive times, its Apocalypse describing the times of the new heaven and earth ; with many varieties of chronicle and biography in between.

3

minute ago or to the happenings in the pre-human age
detected by astronomers, geologists, and biologists.
The popular remark, at a time of crisis, that " we are
making history " is perfectly just. To speak of " pre-
historic times " is, of course, convenient for certain
purposes, as referring to times before written records,
but it is apt to mislead ; for, to the imagination of
science, there is a history that precedes writing. In
spite of divisions and wars, the " spell " of humanity
is the story of one ascent, one struggle, one development of civilization. Pascal said that " The whole
succession of men during the ages should be considered
as one man, ever living and ever learning."[1] Second-
century theology expressed the same general conception
when the writer of Hebrews glanced back at heroic
pioneers and said, " These all died in faith, not having
received the promises, but having seen them afar off,
and were persuaded of them, and embraced them, and
confessed they were strangers and pilgrims on the
earth." In quite another and more modern way,
Auguste Comte uttered the same thoughts when, after
saying that " history is the true guide of human life,"
and remarking that " The living are essentially and
more and more governed by the dead," he also threw
the vision forward in affirming that " Every great soul
always labours for posterity, and refuses to be overmuch absorbed in the present."

The history of humanity should be known to all
mankind. We might say to the whole world what the
inscription over the entrance to the Greek temple said

---

[1] This memorable observation occurs in his unfinished essay,
" Du Vide " (on the vacuum) : and he was speaking of the
continuity of human knowledge.

to every worshipper, " Man, know thyself." Not only should every girl and boy in our own country have reasonably clear conceptions of history, as outlined in the brief table at the opening of this book, but, with adaptations to meet the varied nationalities, all the youth of the civilized world should be taught to reverence the common human past, and to draw inspiration from its examples. Among helps to international fraternity, now openly planned in the League of Nations, this learning of the universal story would not count as the least powerful.

At a great public crisis, Pericles appealed to the Athenians, and, casting about for a strong motive, he found it in history :

> The whole earth is the sepulchre of famous men. Not only are they commemorated by columns and inscriptions in their own country, but in foreign lands there dwells also an unwritten memorial of them, graven not on stone, but in the hearts of men. Make them your examples, and, esteeming courage to be freedom, and freedom to be happiness, do not weigh too nicely the perils of war.

At the close of the Middle Ages an illustrious poet, Dante, and an illustrious educationalist, Vives, brooded on the same theme.   Dante wrote an excellent political essay, in which he said :

> It would be folly to suppose that there is a goal of this civilization or a goal of that, but no one goal of all civilizations. . . . As there is a goal for which nature produces the thumb, and another than this for which she produces the whole hand, and again another than either for which the arm, and another than all these for which the whole man, so there is one goal for which she produces the individual man, another for which the domestic group, another for which the rural district, another for which the city, and another for which the kingdom ; and lastly, there is an ultimate goal for which the eternal God, by His art (which is Nature), brings into being the human race,

in its universality. . . . There is, then, some proper function of
humanity as a whole, for which that same totality of man is
ordained in so great multitude, to which function neither one
man, nor one family, nor one village, nor one city, nor an individual kingdom may attain. . . . The special capacity of
humanity, as such, is a capacity or virtue of intellect. . . . The
speculative intellect, by extension, becomes a practical intellect,
whereof the goal is to do and to make. . . . Universal peace is
the best of all those things which are ordained for our blessedness.[1]

Some two centuries later, the Spanish educationalist,
Vives (1492–1540), thus associated history with the
training of youth :

It is incredible how highly pleasant the study of history is
for right living. How greatly it delights and refreshes the human
soul we see in the old women's fables to which we listen with
close attention and high pleasure, for the sole reason that they
bear upon them some appearance of history. Who, indeed,
does not prick up his ears, and arouse his mind, if he hears any-
thing told which is unusually great, admirable, beautiful, strong ;
a noble deed or saying from those stories of which histories are
so full ? . . . There is nothing of the ancients so worn out by
age, or so decayed, that it may not, in some measure, be accom-
modated to our modes of life. For, although now we may employ
a different form, the usefulness yet remains. . . . In moral
philosophy examples are of more avail than precepts, for every
one more willingly and more promptly imitates what he admires.[2]

Since, in the course of the present study, I shall make
proposals that may appear novel and revolutionary,
I may here observe that, in philosophical effect, I only
aim at what the best types of religious instruction on
the Catholic basis have aimed at. Relatively speaking
—that is, judging the facts in relation to the social
environment and culture-level of the Catholic-feudal
times, and down to the days of Bunyan and Fénelon—

---

[1] " De Monarchia," trans. P. H. Wicksteed. Dante does not
imply that mere peace is blessedness, but that it is a necessary
means.

[2] Foster Watson's translation of " De tradendis disciplinis."

religious instruction pointed to service as the goal, and used history as the source of inspiration. Bible stories, stories of saints, the glowing windows of churches, the carved figures on church walls, the coloured pictures in missals, all represented a sort of universal history and moral evolution in the only forms then possible of comprehension. A small minority of the western Europeans learned the Trivium (the Three-roads-meeting) of grammar, logic, and rhetoric, and the Quadrivium (the Four-roads-meeting) of arithmetic, music, geometry, and astronomy. But those who did had to put their art and science into the same universal frame as was known to the humblest worshippers in church, and their inspiration flowed from the same historical " spell." Necessary things being changed in harmony with twentieth-century needs and outlook in industry and politics, we of to-day should restore this historical method, which a commercial generation and an unimaginative priest-hood have allowed to rust and lapse. If now, I proceed to say—and I say it with earnestness and emphasis— that history should be the central and supreme subject in the instruction of youth, and not a subject of equal rank with a crowd of other subjects, I mean no more, in relation to my century, than did the mediæval teacher of Bible story in relation to his. I add at once that this supreme subject must be rendered the most interesting of all. It should convey the social message to youth. It must carry the educational breath of life. He who makes the message dull plays false to the vital purpose of education. With proper qualifica-tions to the assertion, it may be said that uninteresting instruction is essentially false.

The challenge of life grows stronger. We need a stronger inspiration and a stronger confidence. From history which reveals the facts of man's exploration of nature, of the material basis of society, of industry, of co-operation, of politics, of art, of science, of religion, we may derive the inspiration which creates confidence. There is but one soul—one catholic soul—moving through all this history, crossing seas, fighting famine, clearing forests, growing corn, co-operating in armies or in cities, building political institutions, carrying on commerce, portraying beauty, deducing laws, dedicating itself to an ideal, escaping from disease, cruelty, and ignorance.

> There is a soul above the soul of each,
> A mightier soul, which yet to each belongs.[1]

" All departments of our knowledge," says Comte, " are really component parts of one and the same science—the science of humanity." Hence, we may at the outset ban the time-wasting disputes between the pedants who claim a supreme place for the sciences in education, and the pedants who claim a supreme place for the arts, including noble literature. The complete story of the human soul embraces both the trained appreciation of facts and laws which we call the sciences (all sciences having been slowly built up) and the trained appreciation of art and literature (which have also been slowly built up). These two appreciations are one and the same essential play of the mind, but they are directed to different spheres. Sophie Germain hit upon this truth. In the remark-

---

[1] Opening lines of sonnet, by R. W. Dixon.

able essay, which was published in 1833 (after her death), she said :

Sciences, literature, and the fine arts spring from one and the same sentiment. Each using the means which constitutes its essence, they have reproduced copies, continually renewed, of that inner model and universal type of truth which is so powerfully impressed upon superior minds.

Moments arrive in our experience when it is necessary to abstract the body of thought which we call science, or the body of thought which we call art or literature, from general history. But the history which should take chief rank in education, and to which we should always, after special digressions, return, is the complete drama of industry, research, love of beauty, speech, politics, and visions of the future. Scholars with a gift for analysis can take the poems of Homer and sift out the details, and thus display, in separate compartments, Greek geography, views of nature, social organization, political ideas, religious conceptions, and the rest. This implies that the spiritual historian, whom we call an epic poet, blends all the diverse elements of human culture into one harmonious whole. What poets can do, education should do. Education should use history as a synthesis. At each stage of history the stories and the illustrative hints should indicate the economic activities, the social life, the political life, artistic expression, literary expression, religious expression of the phase studied. A bible, a great picture, a type of craftsmanship, etc., are only truly understood in relation to the age which created them. In that sense there should be no " subjects " in the programme of education. There should be one supreme, inspiring subject, combining all elements, and conveying one call to co-operation and service.

I propose, then, that history should form the central feature of the training of young citizenhood from the kindergarten years to the final studies (if we may dare to call any studies final) of the university, and that all other forms of instruction—moral, civic, religious, æsthetic, intellectual, practical, occupational—should be grouped around, and subordinated to, this central conception of the " One man, ever living and ever learning." And I repeat that, so far from being an impracticable method, it was the method followed by education in the Middle Ages of Europe, not to speak— as one might profitably do—of the similar methods of Judaism, Islam, and Hinduism; only the basis of historical knowledge will, in our modern case, be immensely wider. In our case, again, history will be such as to appeal, not to this or that sect, but to. all schools of thought and faith. The universal alone can appeal to the universal.

From the age of seven to about the age of fourteen the pupils should receive a daily lesson in history : the younger children learning about the Early Age— the Human Genesis—and so on through the world-chronology, with due emphasis on the Motherland ; and, in a liberal spirit, and without attempting rigid niceties, the teacher should bring all the other " subjects "—to use the current term—into closer or remoter relation with the social life and movement of each historical period. As long as this broad principle is accepted, teachers, who differ enormously in bent, taste, and capacity, should be at liberty to construct their own modes of presenting the central theme, and of associating the subordinate topics with the leading motive. After puberty, the principle will still apply, but with larger latitude.

Let me say, at this point, with the utmost frankness, that, so far from wishing to engage in controversy with co-workers in the educational field, I make my plan such that it may give hospitality to all who are offering, or may hereafter offer, contributions of value to the enterprise of youth-training. As I march with my exposition, I may utter an occasional word of dissent, or drop a casual censure ; but, if I were to enumerate the many and admirable efforts now being made for educational progress, I do not think I should reject one as incapable of harmony with my scheme. To tell the truth, I hesitate in calling it " my " scheme. I rather feel it forced upon me by the tendency and genius of the human evolution, and it can clash with no judicious and helpful method devised by modern psychology.

The plan embodied in this book will merge the sacred and the mundane, and seek to obliterate the line between the so-called Religious and the so-called Secular. No theological doctrine will be implied, and no theological references will be shut out. No religious system will be recommended, and no religious system will be ignored. Our " Table of the Early Age " contains the names of six famous communities : Egypt, Babylonia, Greece, Rome, India, China. It is not possible to understand Egypt, Babylonia, Greece, Rome, India, or China, without understanding something of the religion of that country. This " something " can be apprehended by any normal young mind. Children of ordinary intelligence find a joy in seeing the pictures

of Egyptian temples and gods, or of the sacred bulls of
Nineveh, and in hearing the Hindu story of Rama
and Sita, or the story of Buddha or Confucius. All
along the line of history, religious movements and
religious teachers will meet us as intimate elements
of civilization. Each teacher or hero belongs to a
definite age ; and, when young people learn the general
story of that age, they should have spread before them
the vivid presentment of these great personalities as
given in authentic biography or admiring legend.
Mohammed lived and laboured in the Catholic-feudal
Age, and, when that age is studied, in plain and simple
outline, the tale of Mohammed and his disciples should
then be told. John Bunyan was a vital part of England
in the seventeenth century, and, when that century
is reached, the pupils should catch glimpses of the
Pilgrim in his progress. The lessons imparted by this
historical method should be so framed as to win appreciation and respect from all quarters except the hope-
lessly sectarian. To citizens of the British Commonwealth, which embraces a vast variety of religious and
ethical faiths and disciplines, this principle is of immense
importance on political as well as moral grounds. But
to what nation, indeed, is it not of importance ?

The spirit in which I elaborate the present scheme is
entirely consonant with that of Dr. F. H. Hayward's
proposals for school liturgies which would express
national, civic, and social ideals through ceremonial,
music, recital of noble prose and poetry, salutation of
portraits, busts, and emblems, pageant-scenes, etc.,
as integral parts of education, and enacted in a manner
acceptable to all the citizenhood. In all its aspects—
historical, literary, and artistic—the proposal is finely

designed to kindle imagination, touch the heart, and attune young souls with the grandest traditions of our race.[1]

Darwin's " Origin of Species," which prepared the way inevitably for the conception of the "Descent of Man," was published in 1859. During the two generations that have since passed, large groups of educated people have experienced a singular dislocation of thought when, after having been accustomed in earlier years to the idea of a recent creation, they discovered, in the Darwinian literature, that the race was hundreds of thousands of years old. The youth of the future will be spared the labour of such a revision. This will not mean that, in the kindergarten stage, formal mention of the " antiquity of man " will be made. It means that younger children will be habituated, through pictures, songs, dances, folk-lore, handwork, and the rest, to the atmosphere, scenery and objects associated with our primitive fathers. Later stages will reveal history in quite definite periods, which will bear distinctive names. Long before the pupil can tell time accurately, so to speak, by the clock of history, that is, long before he can enumerate the series of Stone Age, Bronze Age, Iron Age, Age of Slavery, Catholic-feudal Age, Age of Expansion, Industrial Revolution, Democratic Age, and the like, he should unconsciously feel that certain phases are later and more developed than others. For example, without reference to a table or book, he would readily place a man in armour at a later point than a skin-clad warrior bearing a bow, just

[1] See Dr. Hayward's and Arnold Freeman's " Spiritual Foundations of Reconstruction : a Plea for New Educational Methods " (P. S. King, 1919) ; and " A First Book of Celebrations," by Dr. Hayward (P. S. King, 1920).

as a child familiar with Bible history, though untaught
in chronology, would think of a king as posterior to a
patriarch like Jacob or Abraham. If, therefore, in
the ensuing pages, I use such terms as " Primitive
man," " Catholic-feudal Age," etc., it does not at
all follow that I would designedly repeat these names of
periods to the young learners ; but I would have the
complexes of ideas that are associated with the great
periods succeed one another in the natural order in the
course of the children's study. And if some reader
should question : " Do you, then, wish the youngest
children to hear exclusively of things primitive, and
elder children to hear exclusively of things modern ? "
I reply, " Assuredly not ; I wish younger children to
hear mainly of earlier things in human industry and
psychology, the teacher having perfect freedom to
superpose modern ideas ; and I wish elder children to
follow the modern records of humanity, the teacher
having perfect freedom to recapitulate the scenes and
messages of the past." Froebel very finely said that
" the child's development as a member of the human
race shows the nature, capacities and tendencies of the
whole of humanity." Let the child be borne, in
imagination, through the Older Testaments and Newer
Testaments of man's soul in due sequence, but always
as a child of to-day, with an intelligence that mirrors
the pageant of to-day as well as of yesterday and the
ancient days.

Permit me now to devote a few pages to the pre-
paratory stage, when the germs of the historical sense
—one might say the filial sense—are implanted in the
mind of the child of five, six, seven, or eight years.

In music, dancing, drama, and poetry, primitive

minds—which in their way, may be as vigorous, and as valid for progress, as modern cultivated minds— love simplicity ; that is, what appears simplicity to us of the later stage.   Mr. Herbert MacIlwaine observed that among Australian savages melodies were sung on three notes only.   Hearing a black fellow chant a mono-tone, accompanied by hand-claps on a log, he inquired, and learned that the subject was the exciting capture that day of a runaway horse.   Such a combination of music and history would be easily understood by our children, far better, indeed, than if the narrative were rendered by an operatic air.   Folk-songs, that is, the people's songs of their daily interests and admirations, are very simple ; and Mr. Cecil Sharp tells us that folk music was the foundation of art music.   Such songs, or songs modelled on them, should form the musical staple for our children.   It is as well to note Mr. Sharp's advice that folk-songs taught to younger pupils should come of their own nationality.   Of folk-dancing, such as the Russian " Isba "—a species of Harvest Feast— a casual mention may suffice, for exercises in this circle of art have already found an honoured place in our kindergartens. So also with what may be called "nature-plays."   These emotions are expressed, again, in the best children's poetry.   A child's repetitions, sometimes continued for an extraordinarily long time in sing-song refrains or original action-chants, do not proceed from sheer love of repetition, but rather from a need for unbroken expression, the monotony being the result of scant ideas and resources.   The likeness to primitive man is obvious.

Since the human intellect has been, to a great degree, built up through its relations with animals, plants, and minerals, education long ago planned instruction in these three fields for young children. When one examines the endless marvels and beauties displayed in a first-rank geological museum, and then thinks how small is the contact of millions of children with these natural wonders, and how many opportunities of mental expansion are thus lost, one longs to spread these treasures straightway before the eyes of the world's youth. The blocks, balls, slabs, beads, etc., which Dr. Montessori and the Froebelians put in front of inquiring children have admirable uses. But when civilization is more generously inclined towards youth, it will freely give it stores of crystals, stones, metals, and sands, not for tedious enumeration of qualities, but to evoke delights of exploration and analysis. The plant-world approaches yet nearer to human sentiments. We rightly use the school-garden for such varied purposes as personal habit-training, æsthetic, and natural economy. We may plan even more deeply. In growing a plant in a pot, the idea of history itself is foreshadowed in the cycle of seed, growth, branches, maturity, seed, and even in variation and the action of environment. The teacher can thus spiritually prepare the way for the conception of evolution. And though the starry heaven is a more appropriate theme for later stages, yet early childhood may be helped to turn its vague wonder into a little knowledge. The stars and planets entered the religious and intellectual sphere at a very early period of history, and a sense of the far grandeur of the skies should be linked with our ripest and profoundest scholarship.

Almost with fear and trembling I touch the subject of mathematics. Education has dealt very cruelly with the child in two fields that are wide apart : religion and mathematics ; though, perhaps, to the eye of philosophy they are much nearer than they seem. Both have been badly reduced to mechanism and rote.   The value of arithmetic—the first step in mathematics—does not essentially lie in its aid to accuracy, as unimaginative teachers have supposed ; accuracy may be enlisted for the most devilish purposes.   The value of arithmetic or calculation, of geometry or measurement, and of mechanics or motion study, lies in evoking a sense of order and harmony in life without and life within—a sense of law and of the need of a reasonable submission of our personal whims to a higher call. If, to certain Greek philosophers, numbers govern the world, and God is the great geometer, surely we modern teachers can make a nobler use of mathematics, even in the primary school, than in the soul-destroying servitude of dreary " sums."   The illustrious J. H. Fabre, who spent a long life in admiration of insect-life and other realms of natural order, expressed his feeling for mathematics in a poem of thirty-seven stanzas, of which the following refers to the heavenly bodies :

> Le nombre, fils du Ciel, le nombre est cet archange,
> Qui chasse devant lui leur ardent phalange,
>   Et du doigt trace leur essor,
> Archange radieux qui sous ses larges ailes,
> Pensif et recueilli, dans ses mains immortelles,
>   Tient le compas aux branches d'or.[1]

[1] " Number, son of Heaven, is the archangel who drives before him the burning host (of planets, etc.), and whose finger traces their course ; the bright archangel who, wide-winged, meditative, and intent, holds, in his immortal hands, the golden-footed compass."   A hint here for a schoolroom picture more inspiring than tables of weights and measures.

Mathematics, indeed, should for the child be twin with æsthetics.

A French traveller asked a village chief in Indo-China how many people had died in a recent plague. The chief, as he called out each victim's name, laid a stick on the ground, saying : " Died during harvest ; died at the beginning of the rains," and adding, as he placed the thirteenth stick, " What a number ! " Not a single native present could assign a name for the total, thirteen.   Such anecdotes may be cited as illustrating the miserable limitations of the primitive intellect.   To me, they are a reminder that the mathematical scope of primitives and children is very narrow ; and they also raise the question whether, within that scope, a great deal of important thinking may not be possible.   Popular talk rightly appreciates the significance of the statement that two and two are four, and rightly employs it as a standing symbol of rationality.   To discern that *one man* and *one tree* are *two things*, is a first step in abstraction, in the sense of equation, in the process of combining.   In the further conception that two and two are four the action is repeated on a higher plane.   This man with two eyes or two feet is seen to resemble the other man with two eyes or two feet.   It is a new equation ; it is the old equation, one and one are two, enlarged ; and perhaps it dimly senses other equations in the future ; and they will duly arrive in the shape of three and three are six, and so on illimitably.   He who gets so far is already a reasoner ; he can combine and compare. Already, in spite of a thousand errors of fancy and magic, he has a basic idea of law, order, harmony, reason, in the world about him.   Already, though so ill able to express his thoughts and intuitions, he feels a kind of evolutionary tap-tap, a first-second, a this-that, a like-and-like, a like-and-unlike, in the wide scene of experience. If so much can happen by the time one reaches four, much more can happen when the growing intellect reaches ten, or, like the Orinoco native, uses " man " as a symbol of twenty (fingers and toes). I conclude that while, of course, the ordinary child will pick up from his social environment all sorts of phrases implying large numbers, even millions, he need not, in the educational exercises of earlier stages, be led beyond a few tens. The sense of logic should be founded rather on a wide range of comparative observations, which do not require the immediate reinforcement of figures. Mr. Benchara Branford[1] has pointed out that young children command an extensive series of ideas such as top, side, bottom, above, below, inside, outside, here, there, shorter, taller, big, little, far, long, broad, thick, thin, solid, point, line, round, half-as-big, and so on. Let the child have an abacus, beads, peas, beans, blocks ; let him have ruler, compass, scales, measuring-string ; give him helps with blackboard sketches, pictures, models ; severely economize figures. Then let him explore among such things as the following, in the study of which he will exercise his mind by tracing, comparing, and noting exceptions and surprises, causes, effects : arches, doors, viaducts, roofs, gables, beams, balls, balances, bridges, barometer, calendar, canals, circles, chains, clocks, drums, inclines, lenses, levers, locks, millstones, mirrors, ploughs, pumps, palings, ships, stairs, shadows, water, water reflections, wheels, etc. Give him objects to classify, and he will

[1] "Study of Mathematical Education" (1908).

unconsciously exercise one of the leading scientific faculties. Indicate to him that lovely aspect of mathematics—the rhythm in dance, music, and poetry. Let him analyse and synthesize ; that is, let him take patterns or certain selected objects to pieces, and piece them together again. Let him copy a pattern with decrease or increase. Let him notice rates of motion, faster, slower, with common-sense calculations of approaches and departures—not without thoughts of road-crossing, and the like. And do not forget, at times, to invite him to measure rivers and mountains !— in other words, let him feel his and your limitations, and how a vast sea of the Impossible girdles our tiny Possible. The poet in " Job," asked :

Canst thou bind the cluster of the Pleiades, or loose the bands of Orion ?   Canst thou lead forth the Mazzaroth in their season, or canst thou guide the Bear with her train ?

Gently, and never brutally, let the child recognize the check of unmodifiable destinies. If, now and then, you bid him make dots on paper or blackboard to represent the pigs or birds you are talking of, you are hinting at the difference of concrete and abstract, and even at metaphysic. I do not imply that these exercises in constructing the mathematical sense should all be formal. Not a few of them can be made incidental to stories.

As to drawing, the teacher may take a hint from his own blackboard method, and from primitive man's method. In each case, drawing is largely used to tell a story, significant features alone are recorded (shading, for example, is seldom introduced), and the work is often little more than symbolical. Children should be encouraged to illustrate a story in their own way, and no matter how crudely. Perhaps chalk and blackboard may afford better instruments, in some cases, than pencil and paper. And let colour—whether in painting or crayoning circles, squares, lines, wheels, quilt patterns, lettering, etc., or examined in the turns of a kaleidoscope, etc.—be presented as a source of joy and exhilaration, and not at all, in the earlier stage, as material for nice discrimination and exact naming of shades.

Elementary symbols, such as the rayed star, or the almanac signs for full moon, crescent-moon, and invisible moon, are easily understood by children ; and young minds will find amusement in deciphering the simpler kinds of picture-writing practised by American Indians, and other tribes of simple culture. No stiff rule can be laid down for learning alphabetic writing. If a child shows desire, let him learn his letters quickly, and read and write quickly. Let him linger, if he so inclines. But let the lingering personage at least be attracted by a first symbol ; and if (suppose) his name is Alfred, let him scratch, or draw, or carve the letter A, which, like some chieftain, he may regard as his very own mark, not without its uses for signature and recognition. The rest will follow in time. So far as suits the convenience of teacher and class-room, show young children how symbols and letters may be stamped in clay, cut on stone or bone, inscribed on waxed or smeared boards,[1] rough-painted with brush or quill, on paper ; in a word, show him the primitive steps. As soon as his understanding is sufficiently enlarged,

---

[1] Beechwood, boc, book ; lino, *litum, litera*, the smear-mark. See Clodd's " Story of the Alphabet " (1900).

choose from travellers' tales any such illustration as this : William Mariner, cast ashore with other Englishmen on the island of Tonga, mixed gun-powder with sticky matter, and with this crude ink scratched a letter which a friendly Tongan promised to give to the captain of any passing vessel. The king, hearing of this unusual action, seized the letter, and compelled one of Mariner's English comrades to interpret. Sending for Mariner, he said, " Put down me on the paper " ; and he was obeyed. A third Englishman was fetched, and was able to read the royal name aloud. The king gazed at the written name in astonishment, crying, " This is not like me ; where are my legs ? "

The amazed king truly resembles the ever-wondering child. And this point may be proper for the observation that we adults have too often credited young children with extraordinary faculties for imagination and fancy, because they stray into singular propositions that amuse us or stagger us, and because they take delight in fairy-tales. The average child is not at all imaginative. It simply pieces together, in a crude and —what is frequently to us—comic manner the odds and ends of its ideas ; but this haphazard process is vastly different from the genuine imagination which, with a genius akin to that of science, frames new worlds out of the materials of experience. A child's eager attention to the miracles of the fairy-tale is nothing more than the primitive man's wonder, shallow and swiftly-passing, at the medley of objects and changes presented by any unaccustomed scenes and incidents. Neither the Primitive nor the child dwells in a romantic spiritual world of which civilization or adulthood robs the innocent soul. The dazed and superficial wonderment, it is true, is a healthy initiation into a profounder mental life, but it is not a condition to be envied or prolonged. No sane child wants to return to it.

The preliminary reflections into which I have invited the reader will apply to the kindergarten stage of education, but it is obvious that some of them have over-run that stage, and anticipated ideas and exercises that belong to ensuing periods.

Before proceeding to outline the course of the Story of Humanity, which should furnish the main thread of instruction for ages six or seven to fourteen or fifteen, it may be well to lay down a dual proposition. The awakening of good feeling should be the first aim of the educator, and the training of the intelligence— without which good feeling is not effectively awakened —is secondary. This dual proposition, taught to us by the whole record of civilization, holds true all through primary education, secondary, and university. Without normal sympathies, neither genuine service of the commonwealth is possible nor genuine industry.

For example, in describing the condition of Early mankind, cave-dwellers and fire-discoverers, the teacher may tell the noble legend of Prometheus, who tamed the fire from heaven,[1] taught man the use of animals and the healing virtues of plants, and suffered the pains which all suffer who mould morality and culture to greater values, and win progress by forethought. Or she may

[1] Why say " stole " ?

And he tamed fire which, like some beast of prey,
Most terrible, but lovely, played beneath
The frown of man.
        (Shelley : " Prometheus Unbound.")

tell the legend of the cave of one-eyed Polyphemus, and the escape of ingenious Ulysses and his companions ; nor forget to call in the aid of many delightful fairy-tales and scraps of folk-lore which lend romance to the cave. Even Plato's cave and its wonderful shadows may be lightly hinted at in a simple picture, without, of course, any attempt to interpret the parable. In short, the child's interest, quickened by the teacher's imagination, should be enlisted from the outset on the side of human courage, hope, quest, co-operation, service.

Both for teacher and child, a recital of the story of the Human Genesis involves a splendid intellectual exercise. The interest of the fairy-tale, told in a modern spirit, is mainly picturesque and emotional, and its unrestrained play of fancy is not expected to train the intellect. But in spelling out the tale of the history of human happenings, teacher and child have to reconstruct scenes and situations, and to get at a real harmony of means and ends. For example, as to reconstruction, take Professor Breasted's picture of the discovery of metal, 4000 B.C. :

Some Egyptian once happened to bank his camp fire with pieces of copper ore lying on the ground about the camp. The charcoal of his wood fire mingled with the hot fragments of ore piled around to shield the fire, and thus the ore was " reduced," as the miner says ; that is, the copper in metallic form was released from the lumps of ore. Next morning, as the Egyptian stirred the embers, he discovered a few glittering globules, now hardened into beads of metal. He drew them forth, and turned them admiringly as they glittered in the morning sunshine. Before long, as the experience was repeated, he discovered whence those strange shining beads had come. He produced more of them, at first only to be worn as ornaments by the women. Then he learned to cast the metal into a blade, to replace the flint knife which he carried in his girdle.[1]

[1] J. H. Breasted's " Ancient Times " (1916).

Even if, in the form here given, the exercise in reconstructing an incident in discovery (that is, science) is beyond the capacity of young children, it furnishes an excellent type of the mental action needed in picturing-out history as distinguished from legend and fairy-tale. So also in judging human motives. Whereas, in the fairy-tale, all sorts of grotesque creatures appear and perform marvels, the facts in Primitive History must rationally cohere. Early man, with very limited tools, and with but a few domesticated animals, can only produce limited effects, and young learners must school their thought in simple calculations of what he could or could not do. The intellectual discipline thus begun will be expanded and strengthened all through the study of history. No error could be more foolish than to class observation of human motives and deeds as less intellectual in quality than observation of facts in the physical world.

It will be convenient to divide our material, as in the prefatory table, into three stages: Early, Catholic-feudal, and Expansion. The reader must pardon occasional and strong abbreviation on the ground that a concise summary best gathers up the significance of such vast periods. I shall, at times, break into anecdote, and I shall now and then illustrate the method by giving notes of lessons. Let it also be understood that I shall only trace the History of Humanity in so far as, broadly speaking, it may fall within the comprehension of young people. And, further, let it be understood that the wealth of detail is purposely made much too full for management by any one teacher, or any one series of class-teachers. One type of teacher will prefer such and such material, another will select differently. But all should follow the same general chronology. I trust the repetition is not wearisome if I again say that, if one may term this history scheme a " subject," then this subject will be the sole substance of the instruction through a school-life from the age of six, seven, or eight (it is best to speak loosely) to the age of fourteen or fifteen.

CHAPTER II

EARLY AGE

(TO ABOUT A.D. 400)

IN talking about Primitive man to young children, we must avoid stressing the brutish qualities, both because history is the tale of our secular escape from brutishness, and because immature minds cannot bear the weight of the full truth. Giants and monsters, indeed, do not frighten the normal child ; he loves their dramatic sensation. But the central element must be genial and companionable. One could not have a better type of method than the admirable myth of Heracles, who engages in masterly combat, for social ends, against reptiles, stinks, and other forms of anarchy.

If we picture Early man at the point where the family, in however rude a guise, has become the social basis, we can safely add the shadowy facts of tribal wars, exploitations, and slavery in an outer circle of narrative. The Hebrew Biblical legends follow this principle ; so also does the Hindu " Ramayana," which paints so stirring a portrayal of ancient life and manners, and while freely admitting the demons, puts domestic love and friendship in the centre.[1] Here, then, is our syllabus of the history of the Early Age :

[1] The story is told, in child language, in my " Divine Archer " (Dent & Son).

Glimpses of Primitive man in cave or forest ; hints at varieties of types, as in long-heads and broad-heads (children can amuse themselves by measuring one another's heads), etc.

Sketch of Wookey Hole in Somersetshire, or any similar cave ; tree-dwellers of China ; huts ; pile-dwellings of Switzerland, or later Borneo. Simple pictures of Australian black fellows, their clans, totems of kangaroo, snake, etc. Varieties of clothing—a subject on which a teacher with delicate ingenuity can pass beyond the mere curiosities of savage and barbaric dress ; for, as Comte has said, " Clothing was the earliest real step in that noble discipline which man has instituted for the direct improvement of his own nature, by a continuous repression of his coarsest and strongest instincts." Stories of Adam and Eve, Athene in armour, etc.

Fire ; preparation of food. Weapons and tools of stone, bronze, iron, this threefold chronology being carefully adhered to. Hunting, agriculture, shepherding, and the associated legends. Logs as floats, dug-outs made by fire, reed-rafts of Nile, rafts on inflated skins, canoes. Ark stories. Animals, as seen in legend, and in more exact nature-study, and mainly confining the descriptions to animals known to the Early Age—dog, ox, sheep, goat, pig, horse, ass, camel, elephant, cat (linking the domesticated creatures with ideas of kindness and gratitude), lion, tiger, ape, wolf, eagle, vulture, owl, woodpecker, hawk, crow, peacock, swan, cock, tortoise, crocodile, serpent, bee (economic importance of honey ; Biblical " milk and honey," etc.), fly, locust, grasshopper, scarab-beetle ; add mythic creatures, such as centaur, griffin, medusa (octopus), and delightful dragons in general ; the wit and wisdom of Æsop, and perhaps something from La Fontaine.

Colonel G. E. Church, in his interesting work on the " Aborigines of South America," remarks on the influence of the horse upon the modes of life of the Pampean tribes. " They found that he greatly facilitated the food quest, made it possible to concentrate the tribal sections into masses, and to make tribal combinations for war which, with his aid, could be carried to far outlying regions which they had never before penetrated. Their little home properties and tent comforts could be increased, and were no longer impedimenta on the march. To invent or acquire these wakened their dormant intellectual powers. The horse, in fact, caused the Indian to extend his lines of thought, learn something of the life and habits of distant peoples, exchange ideas with them, plunder or trade with them ; in short, take the initial steps in civilization." Colonel Church adds : " Without the aid of the horse, it may be doubted if mankind could have emerged from barbarism, and when his strength was utilized to move the wheel and axle (the greatest invention ever made) civilization was assured."

For quite another aspect of human relations with domestic animals, note this from C. Holdenby's " Folk of the Furrow " :

" I had always thought Fred, the carter, the most uncouth fellow on the farm. He had something of the step of his mares in his gait, his eye had just their glance, he even spoke in a kind of whinny. One of his team fell ill ; the man was night and day with the mare, tending its every whim. Once I came suddenly into the stable and found Fred with her nose in his two hands, and his face right up against the beast's cheek. He was talking to it in a kind of soothing undertone, and the mare just whimpered back. His face had a life about it that I had never noted before ; there was a sympathy and expression beyond what I had ever imagined, and I knew all at once that Fred was a born carter."

These two quotations have a significant bearing on Primitive Sociology, and suggest considerations additional to the ordinary " kindness to animals " motive.

Plants—millet, rye, oats, barley, wheat, rice, beans, lentils, carrot, onions, turnip, cucumber, cabbage, sugar (Isaiah xliii, 24 ; Jeremiah vi, 20), tea, olive, vine, fig, date, almond, chestnut, apple, pomegranate, apricot, pear, cherry, plum, mulberry, bamboo, oak, ivy, incense, hemp, flax, cotton, indigo.[1] Some of these vegetable products have had an enormous influence on Early (as on subsequent) civilization, and some, such as the vine and olive, play great parts in myth, folk-lore, poetry, and religion. Minerals—gold, silver, tin, copper (bronze), iron, lead, flint, marble, salt, etc., salt being highly important as connected with both food and pottery :

> Thales, the first name in Greek philosophy, was, among his other activities, a salt merchant, just as Plato, two hundred years later, dealt in oil. (Marvin's " Living Past.")

Village and industry ; stone-chipping, grinding ; carving of stone, wood, ivory, bone ; pottery ; metal-work, metal mirrors ; ploughs first drawn by man, later by oxen (the plough-theme one of the greatest in social evolution and literature), simple mechanical powers.

> An ingenious story-teller might find, in the island of Crete (one of the most important places in history), and its environment, a singular complex of myth and what may be called industrial lore : Daedalus (Greek, *daidalos*, skilled worker, artist, artificer), who, with his nephew, makes axes, awls, bevels, saws (copied from the chin-bone of a snake), potter's wheel, lathe, plummet, glue, wooden images with outstretched limbs, ship-sails (the wings of Icarus), and the Cretan labyrinth ; Talus, the brass giant ; the chalk (cretaceous) rocks, yielding the " creta " used by Roman teachers. Add the cave of Zeus, the golden sceptre of the judge Minos, the passage of ships to and from Athens, the story of Theseus, and the numerous objects, turned up by twentieth century excavation, revealing the social scene of ancient Crete ; and you have material for many-sided lessons, brimming with interest.

Property : first ideas of " mine " and " thine " ;

---

[1] See A. de Candolle's " Origin of Cultivated Plants " and Dr. Rendel Harris's curious notes in " The Ascent of Olympus."

barter and trade, as illustrated in Herodotus's account of the Carthaginian merchants exchanging clothing, etc., for the gold of West African negroes. Co-operation, a vital subject, the thread of which should be traced from Primitive co-operation in food-gathering, hunting, agriculture (and even in the discipline exacted in war), right through the ages to the vast co-operative enterprises of to-day. Along this economic line, we shall arrive at a medium of exchange, first in *pecunia*, cattle, etc., and then in Cretan coins, Lydian (Asia) coins, and the civic treasure of Athens, embodied in the statue of Athene, overlaid with gold, which served as the public and collective store for emergency.

The story of war cannot be avoided, either in history, legend, or fairy-tale. Even at this early point in education, the teacher, while avoiding premature discussion, can subordinate the bloodshed element, and stress the elements of discipline, co-operation, public spirit, courage, and heroism for service. The origin of slavery, in reserving captives for industry instead of slaughter after battle, is quite comprehensible by children, and it is very important historically.

On the lighter side, we shall note magic in fairy-tales and general folk-lore, or in survivals such as beliefs connected with the horseshoe, spilling the salt, and the like, all of which are to be dealt with smilingly, and without any hint at serious study. Add old customs of May Day dances and Jack-in-the-Green, midwinter feasts, and midsummer fires, helpful for seasonal and calendar observations as well as for enlivening anecdote. Sir J. G. Frazer's monumental volumes on " The Golden Bough," primarily designed for students of sociology, will yield to the teacher no small amount of entertaining and instructive materials. On the popular side, the tale of Brer Rabbit, and similar bits of folk-lore, African and other, will sketch primitive notions of life, manners and the animal world. Here also we get the aid of the folk-songs diligently collected and adapted by such researchers as Cecil J. Sharp. Concrete themes of these songs are " Sly Reynard, " The Frog," " The Crow," " Robin-a-thrush," and the like. The psychology of the folk-song merits the close study of teachers. Mr. Sharp's remark that " The folk-song is communal, and reflects the feelings and tastes that are communal rather than personal," is significant. Observe also the constant presence of a simple, obvious, and whimsical type of humour, much appreciated by children, as in the ending of a song :

> This song it was made for gentlemen,
> If you want any more, you must sing it again.

I have previously referred to the meaning of such joyous repetition. In this sphere of vocal music I suspect a good deal of instruction could be drawn from a sympathetic examination of the songs popular among coloured people in the United States.

Our " History Table " names Egypt, Babylon, India, China, and we may attach Phœnicia on the west, and Japan on the east, and Persia midway. I am far from harbouring any such frightful proposition as that children aged eight or ten should be buried under systematic accounts of these nations. We do not overwhelm the young people who con the old Hebrew stories, when we also tell the tale of Esther, and thus introduce Persia to our stage. And, in just that elementary way, I think that, having given first impressions of Early man, we should next impart a group of impressions of life, manners, and environment in Egypt, Babylon, etc., each teacher omitting or including topics as may seem advisable. Only on that clear understanding, the following notes are presented : The part played by great rivers, Blue and Yellow Rivers in China, Ganges and Indus in India, Tigris and Euphrates in Babylonia, Nile in Egypt. Egypt : pyramids, mummies, statues, looms, pottery, copper, tools, needles and weapons ; ships, sails, helm, oars, mast, holed stone for anchor (rudder unknown till the Middle Ages) ; symbolic eyes in front of vessel ; Egyptians the first people to meet the Black man. Phœnician merchants and sailors, some of whom, in ships with bows showing birds' heads and two big eyes, even penetrated to China ; Chinese imitations of these ships. Japanese junks cross to America. India should be pictured mainly through its noble epics, the " Ramayana " and " Mahabharata," and folk-tales.[1] Babylonia, its palm-trees, sculptures, book-tablets, Creation-story, etc. At this stage, the big-eyed ships have more than an interest of oddity. They represent the spirit of exploration and commerce, of caravans over deserts, of Phœnician quests in the North for tin and amber, of Ulysses in his wanderings, of the Cretan Minos who (as Thucydides tells) endeavoured to clear the sea of pirates. And as we recite the tales of this period, we shall let it appear that, in this wider world, the old patriarchs are displaced by

---

[1] The " Ramayana " is told in very simple language in my " Divine Archer." Dent's " Everyman Library " contains Dutt's selections of the two epics in verse. Many Eastern stories, including Hindu, are given in my " Youth's Noble Path " (Longmans). See also Miss Noble's " Cradle-Tales of Hinduism " (Longmans).

kings. So far as the children's capacity for reading maps may allow, we shall draw extremely simple maps of the Mediterranean region, with shadowy outlines of a world beyond. Maps modelled in sand on a large floor-space would be better still. This map will grow wondrously from school-year to school-year.

Our syllabus now recurs to science and letters :

Mathematics : the whole object, at this stage, being to establish a foundation-interest in number and measure as a means of intellectual, social, and artistic order. Long before " sums " are thought of, interests should cluster round numbers as such : (1) The single, the alone, the pioneer, the solitary watch. (2) Two, twain, twin, twice, scales, pair, couple, double, hands, arms, wings, marching steps. (3) Three, thrice, trio, triangle trefoil, tripod, parents-and-child. (4) Four winds, four seasons, cross-roads of Hermes, square, quadruped. (8) Notes of the scale. (10) Fingers, as basis of Roman notation. Number associated with petals, crystals, stars, chequer-patterns, and rhythms in music, dancing, poetry. Colours should be freely enlisted for counters, patterns (as in playing-cards), abacus, the chequer-board (as in Egyptian Table, or Table of Pythagoras, up to $9 \times 9 = 81$, or the later Table up to $12 \times 12 = 144$). Sharing among companions, as in cutting an apple, and the like, should be the first adventure in " fractions." The primitive notched stick should have a place. Measuring should begin, as in the case of Early man, with the rough-and-ready use of the cubit (elbow to finger-tip), span, palm, foot ; string or rope as measures. Weighing in the balances with its ideas of evenness, addition, subtraction. Simple geometrical conceptions should never open from rigid blackboard figures, but be drawn from common objects, such as rods, sticks, boxes, books, chests, trays, balls, eggs, windows, flags, pavements, etc., and they should frequently be connected with colours. In short, the mathematical foundations should be laid in æsthetic, and the morning-stars of art should sing together, when the corner-stone of logic (for mathematic is logic), is established. For ordinary children (one can exclude precocious calculators) simple arithmetical exercises up to 100 should be concerned with concrete, familiar, and often amusing objects, avoiding the cruelty of the mechanical " sums " which confuse the mind rather than make for accuracy ; and the aim should be, above all, to foster a cheerful sense of world-order and social order.

A London journal, in 1918, related how an instructor in workshop arithmetic had no little trouble in convincing a young mechanic that there were one hundred hundredths in an inch. He next asked his pupil how many thousandths he reckoned there would be in an inch. After gazing long and earnestly at his ruler, the youth uttered a mild oath, and said " There must be *millions* of 'em ! " The youth had probably done many " sums " in his school-days, and yet had never learned to (if one may put it so) respect figures.

This respect for figures, again, should, in the case of children, be based directly upon respect for household and social order, as in careful reckoning of money in family accounts, etc., and not on an irrelevant awe of accuracy as such. It has been sensibly observed by W. T. Sheppard, that " The value of arithmetic has usually been regarded as consisting in the stress it lays on accuracy. The development of physical science has tended to emphasize the exactly opposite aspect, namely, the impossibility, outside a certain limited range of subjects, of ever obtaining absolute accuracy, and the consequent importance of not wasting time in attempting to obtain results beyond a certain degree of approximation." (Article " Arithmetic," in " Encyclopædia Britannica.")

The existence of Leap Year in our calendar ought to check pride in human arithmetic !

First notions of the calendar : sunrise, sunset, differing

lengths of daylight, varying positions of sun, sundials, hours, clocks of water-drops or running sand, hour glass, shadows, moon, months, weeks, years. (The 365-day calendar was invented by Egyptians, 4241 B.C.) Father Time, Aurora, etc.[1]

Alphabet, picture-writing of Red men, etc. (Children tend to picture-writing spontaneously.) Peruvian symbolization of soldiers by red strands, gold by yellow, silver by white, corn by green ; one knot in cord for ten, two knots for twenty. Show a few striking Egyptian hieroglyphics. Even at this stage, devices may be used to interest the children in language as such, e.g., in noting the imitative character of certain words : " cuckoo," " bang," " roar " ; or a few French words may be learned by way of, not task, but entertainment.[2]

Hebrew history and legends, including selected stories from the Apocrypha, such as " Tobit " and " Judas Maccabæus " ; and stories of Rabbis.

The Greeks, largely presented through pictures, and stories from Homer, Herodotus, Plutarch, and the more famous myths (Heracles, Prometheus, Demeter, Jason). Scenes from the siege of Troy should come first, and then should come hints of a great sea-life in ships manned by slaves, the wanderings of Ulysses, etc.[3] The voyage

---

[1] An approach to the human and picturesque method here advocated is made in Professor D. E. Smith's " Number Stories of Long Ago." Illustrated by coloured as well as black-and-white pictures, it traces the arithmetical modes of Egypt, Babylonia, Rome, India, etc., in a simple and lively manner (Ginn & Co., 1920).

[2] At all stages of the subject of language, a teacher may derive instructive hints from an Esperanto dictionary.

[3] See Walter Leaf's " Homer and History " (1915), as to the great Greek migrations.

of Pytheas of Marseilles (third century, B.C.) along
the British coast deserves a brief sketch. Many
incidents in the Persian War, Battle of Salamis, etc.,
as splendidly narrated by Herodotus, can be followed
by children. It is worth while telling this story, for it
furnishes a grand type of civilization defending itself
by wars which, apart from such high motives, would be
unmixed and deplorable evils. Glimpses of games,
dancing, theatres. A few anecdotes of men of science :
Pythagoras listening to the rhythm of a blacksmith's
hammer, the death of Archimedes, etc. Slave-labour
in agriculture, etc. No suggestion of " lessons " on
slavery is here intended ; but it is important in dealing
with Greek, Roman, and other Early histories, to keep
the figure of the slave in evidence ; otherwise immense
misunderstandings may be a drag on the mind, perhaps
permanently.

Romans : free use of pictures ; stories from Virgil
and Plutarch ; legends of Curtius, Horatius, etc.
Social customs. Food included pigeons, thrushes,
peacocks, quails, geese, ducks, fatted mice. Roads,
concrete, baths, canals, aqueducts, basilicas (pictures
of these shown in preparation for Christian churches).
Workmen's clubs and gilds, club-feasts. Holidays,
some fifty a year. (Daubeney's " Roman Husbandry.")

During the Great War, Italian soldiers met peasants in the
" Rumene " (Roman) villages of Albania, whose talk was
sufficiently Latin to be understood. Mr. Lewis R. Freeman
thus describes the soldiers at engineering work :
" If the Italian has something of the feeling of one coming
again to his own in meeting the Rumene of Albania, imagine
to what depths he is stirred when he finds that the easiest grades,
which the precise instruments of his engineers indicate should
be followed in surmounting a lofty mountain range, coincide to
the fraction of a degree with those run by the engineers of
Augustus and Hadrian ; what must be his pride when he sees

that the old Roman bridges—with the great stones of abutment and coping eroded smooth with the wind and rain of 2,000 years, but otherwise intact—are deemed fit to bear the surging traffic of what must be one of the most sorely tried of all the great war roads ! How he is moved in spirit by all of this, how the soul of the ancient Roman awakes again in the modern one, may be judged from the words of an officer of engineers to whom I had expressed my amazement and admiration at the tremendous amount of labour which had been expended on the embanking of a sharp bend where the Santa Quaranta road zig-zagged up the steep range behind Delvino :

' The explanation is very simple,' he said. ' Those huge stones at the bottom of the embankment were probably laid by the Phœnicians (Phœnece is the old name of Delvino), while there is no doubt that the next ten feet of courses were laid by the Romans. Well, that being so, it would indeed be a shameful thing on my part if I failed to make the superstructure worthy of the foundation.' "

And he adds :

" But it is not only the works of old Rome which stir a senti-mental interest in Southern Albania in the breast of the Italian, for it was in this region also that those sturdy navigators, the Venetians, pushed farther from the sea than anywhere else. Following an ancient custom of theirs, every trans-Adriatic colonist was given a gold coin for every olive tree that he planted ; the consequence being that in the vicinity of Vallona alone, the centuries-old veteran trees, that date from the Venetian occupa-tion, may be numbered by the hundreds of thousands." (Article in " Land and Water," September, 1917). This quotation, except the olive-tree item, will not appeal directly to children, but it gives teachers an excellent illustration of one of the main themes of this book—the concatenation, or enchainment, of the historical ages.

The Roman story, even if one simply depended upon Plutarch, yields a most important complex of social and political ideas : family, city, kings, republic, colony, empire, conquest, tyranny, tribute, leagues, treaties, senator, vote, committee, city fire, and watch-ing vestals ; augurs who, on behalf of the public, observed lightning, etc. (physics), and the priests who observed livers, etc. (anatomy), and slavery. Similar conceptions, of course, will have been noted in telling Greek stories.

The following description (in the "Metamorphoses" of Apuleius, second century) of a barrack in which were herded the slaves of Roman millers and bakers is not for children but teachers should bear it in mind : "O gods ! What a city of stunted men I saw there. Their skins were seamed all over with marks of the lash. Their scarred backs were shaded rather than covered with tattered frocks ; some had only aprons ; and all were so clothed that their skin was visible through the rents in their rags. Their foreheads were branded with letters. Their heads were half shaved. They had irons on their legs. They were hideously sallow. Their eyes were bleared, and sore, and raw from the smoke of the ovens, and they were covered with flour, as athletes are with dust when they contend in the arena."

The Christian story, as given in gospels, Acts of the Apostles, and selections from other writings, such as the "Shepherd of Hermas." Add the beautiful story of St. Christopher, and stories of St. Nicholas, patron saint of children, scholars, travellers, and merchants (Santa Claus) ; St. Augustine, in a glimpse only ; St. Jerome, with his lion and writing-table. Perhaps one might recite Jerome's anecdote, characteristic of the time when Catholicism was spreading, of the old Roman Albinus listening with pleasure to the "Alleluias" of his little granddaughter. So far as the present educational scheme is concerned, this group of religious stories can be, and should be, related with such discrimination and sympathy, and such regard for the moral essentials, as to render them interesting and valid to children associated with all types of thought and faith. We have already accepted the same principle in our treatment of the epics of India and the Hebrew scriptures.

Lastly, we may cover a wide field represented by nature-study, first steps in scientific habit (not formal "science"), and practical school activities. The following list of topics, objects, and exercises is related to

the life and environment of the Early Age : Simple
observation of stars, such as the Great Bear ; phases
of moon ; light (" What is darkness ? " asked Aristotle),
rainbow, echo, wind, and weather[1] ; water-power,
waves, tide, ice, well-digging ; the first lighthouse,
or Pharos at Alexandria. Simple view of animal and
plant life ; frogs, newts, worms, butterflies, bees, ants,
wasps, birds, rabbits. Garden-plots, with individual
children's work, and collective work by a group.
Photographs of wild life, as in the researches of Kearton
and Dugmore. Slight glimpses of the microscope,
and, in general, chats on the animals, plants, and
minerals enumerated in this Early Age section, putting
the chief accent, of course, on those of most economic
and social importance, such as ox, sheep, goat, horse,
bee, olive, vine, flax, barley, copper, iron, salt. Pictures
should be abundantly in evidence for architecture, for
scenery (e.g., Turner's " Lake Avernus ") ; and such
symbolic subjects as Ford Madox Brown's beautiful
" Poetry " (Homer), " Philosophy " (Aristotle),
" Oratory " (Cicero) at Manchester, and the Biblical
illustrations by Millais, Burne Jones, Doré, William
Blake, and the Old Masters. Lantern and kinema
should be freely available for this, and every other,
educational stage. The children's theatre, that is
kindergarten plays, dialogues, recitations, and simple
tableaux ; nature games, dances, and songs. Shadow
games, which appeal to children, must often have
amused Primitive man.

With blackboard and coloured chalks, teachers of a certain
turn of mind will even borrow hints from Aristophanes' " Frogs."

[1] Note the beautiful symbolic designs of the Eight Winds on
the " Tower of the Winds " at Athens.

Here is a verse of the Frogs' Song, with the chorus " Brek-kek "
of the males, and the soft chorus " Co-ax " of the females :

> " Loud and louder our chant must flow,
> Sing, if ever ye sang of yore,
> When, in sunny and glorious days,
> Through the marshes and marsh-flags springing,
> On we swept in the joy of singing
> Myriad-diving roundelays.
> *Brek-ek-ek-kex !*
> *Ko-ax, ko-ax !* "

I am not proposing that children should have a lesson on
Aristophanes, but that humour should brighten " nature-study."

Simple gymnastics, with picture-glimpses of Greek
games (with such stories as that of Atalanta and the
three golden apples), and, perhaps, of modern displays,
such as the popular celebrations in Bohemia. In the
field of drawing, measuring, clay-modelling, and the
like : ruler, compass, protractor, set-square, scales,
circle, sphere, Solomon's " Molten Sea " (circular basin),
cone, cylinder, lines, angles, triangles (shamrock, and
similar emblems), square, chain, plumb-line ; Primitive,
conical huts ; mud dome, propylon, pillar, obelisk,
piles, fences, pyramid, Roman arch, pointed brick
arch (Syrian) ; beaker, vase, stone and bronze knives,
stone hammers ; bow and arrow, spear, sword, helmet,
chariot, Roman standards ; drum, top, lyre ; cross,
swastika ; abacus ; Roman letters and figures ; wedge
and arrow-heads. One may recall Professor P. Geddes's
proposal that in public parks children should be allowed
the use of an enclosure for hut-building and the like.

The whole of the present chapter to this point has
been a gradual construction of an extensive Early Age
complex of motives, ideas, and exercises. I have
already stated that no one teacher, and no series of
class-teachers in any one school, could be expected, or
should dream of attempting, to cover so large an area

of instruction. It is merely proposed that, from this complex, or circle of thought and interest, the instruction-material and associated activities of younger children should be derived, with the customary regard to local needs and the pupil's capacities, and with such supplementary references to modern life and manners as the teacher may think helpful to, and harmonious with, the scheme. Reading, writing, and arithmetic should be linked with the topics of this complex ; and, in any case, these three " subjects " are but auxiliaries to great educational and social ends, and have no strong significance in earlier years. If individual boys and girls exhibit a genuine pleasure in any of these three " subjects," let them have a reasonably free scope. Anybody who examines the list of exercises recently enumerated will have no ground for complaining that " self-activity " and " self-development " (if one must use the jargon of certain academic sects) are neglected. But, in this earlier stage, as also in the University and in social and civic life, the chief aim of the teaching of children and students, and of church or platform, should be to summon souls to service in family and country, to give lustre to industry as a process of nature-exploitation, to encourage each personality to express itself through serviceable industry, and to induce all souls to respond to the call of the widest circle of humanity. By the time education reaches the adolescent, this aim will be explicit. In the case of younger learners, it will be implicit ; that is to say, the moral educator will avoid moralizing.

I proceed to lay before the reader three lessons which I have actually given. The report in each case is more concise than the living address, but the general spirit is adequately conveyed. They are not lessons suited to the Early stage treated of in this chapter. But they contain certain basic elements which I have allotted to earlier instruction in the preceding syllabus. They show the chronology of ages, and the enchainment of ages, which, I think, should be salient features in historical instruction. They show that, when we have arrived at the Modern stage of history, our latest ideas have a greater value through being founded on the Early Age complex and the Catholic-feudal, or Mediæval, complex. They also attempt to represent, in a simple way, the principle of synthesis ; that is, the production of a complex in which geography, literature, history (in the usual sense), and hints at ideals are blended together—for life and experience blend them together. Finally, and perhaps paradoxically, I do not recommend these lessons as examples to be systematically followed. Their sweep through centuries, in such brief talks, is somewhat artificial. I beg the reader, therefore, to accept them as symbols of the logic, or general order, of historical thought, which this book advocates. In each case, the map is not placed on the blackboard ready-made at the outset. It grows as the teacher proceeds.

I. LESSON ON INDIA

A prince named Rama walked with his brother in a king's garden, where peacocks spread their tails, and many a lotus lily grew in a lake. Behind trees Rama heard a jingling.

" I know of a surety," said he, " that there comes hither

a lady whom I shall love beyond all things else in the world."

Then appeared the lady Sita, wearing on her ankles jingling silver bangles. She was the king's daughter. And Sita and Rama loved each other then, and for ever.

Sita's father promised to give her in marriage to any prince who could bend the great bow of the god Siva. Many proud kings tried and failed, but Rama bent it till it broke, and the vast crowd of Indians cheered his wondrous strength. Then Rama married Sita amid much music, and took his bride home to the city of Oude. (*Mark a dot for the city.*)

One day, the King of Oude, looking in a polished mirror, saw one of his hairs gone white.

" I am growing old," he said ; " I will make Rama king in my stead."

The citizens hung out banners, and fixed jewels on boughs to look like fruit on trees in the streets, for joy that Rama was king. But the king had two wives, and one was mother to Rama, and another was mother to Prince Bharat.

" O, King," said Bharat's mother, " you once promised to give me any two boons I asked."

" Yes."

" Then I ask two boons : one, let Bharat be king ; two, let Rama go into exile afar off for fourteen years."

He wept in grief, but he kept his word. Next daybreak, Rama and Sita, clad in poor garments, went forth, followed by many sorrowing folk till they came to the River Ganges (*mark Ganges, and outline Indian coast*), and the three wanderers—for Rama's brother joined them—bade farewell to the people. So they travelled and dwelt in the jungle, being friendly with elephants, tigers, lions, monkeys, boars, deer, and birds. For years they thus passed life, crossing the Nilgiri Hills (*mark*) and going always south. A band of horrid demons attacked them once, and Rama shot arrows from his bow—the bow of the god Vishnu—and slew them in heaps. When this came to the ears of the King of Demons in the Isle of Ceylon (*mark*), he plotted a cruel blow. He rode in a chariot, seized the

Lady Sita, and carried her to his island, and Rama's heart was like to break. Armies of people that loved him came to his aid—monkey-folk, and bear-folk, rough to see, and warm in friendship—and the huge host came to the sea, built a bridge, and entered Ceylon. Battles were fought, arrows flew so thick that they darkened the sky. Rama gained the victory with his bow, his faithful low-caste monkeys, his faithful low-caste bears ; and, at the end of the fourteen years, seated in a chariot drawn by flying swans, he and his wife returned through the air to the city of Oude ; and elephants trumpeted, flags waved, drums throbbed, and all the city was glad.[1]

You remember the bow of Siva. Now, the Indian people say that this great Person has his head among mountains, and ice and snow cover his head and shoulders, and from this mountain-head the melting snow runs down and makes the Ganges. (*Mark Himalayas.*) When Siva rides abroad, he sits on an old bull, which, old as it is, Siva yet loves as his servant. Greatly the Hindus honour the bull ; and they think the milk-giving cow a sacred animal, and wreathe her neck with flowers.

Across these mountains of the west came troops of soldiers who honoured the prophet Mohammed. In a battle with the Hindus, a Mohammedan boy, aged thirteen, stood over a fallen Indian, and his friends bade him kill a captured chief. But the boy Akbar said, " How can I strike a man who is as good as dead ? " This noble lad became the famous Emperor Akbar. Black were his eyes and brows, and a wart spotted his nose. On horse or elephant he went hunting with his soldiers. He was a just man to Hindus and Mohammedans, taxing all alike. He dwelt in the cities Delhi, Agra, and Baroda. (*Mark.*) Once he sat in the twilight of dawn on a stone in the court-yard of his palace, and he watched the sun rise over the

---

[1] This is a faint outline of the popular Hindu epic, " The Ramayana." See my " Divine Archer."

" Perhaps," observe Margaret Noble and A. K. Coomara-swami in " Myths of the Hindus," " one might say that no one unfamiliar with the story of Rama and Sita can be a true citizen of the world."

mountains, plains, rivers, and temples of India, and the
sight was most beautiful ; and he said, " I gaze on this
great miracle—the world."[1]

You remember the monkeys and bears who so faithfully
served Prince Rama. I called them the low castes, for the
old poets, I suppose, meant common, rough folk who yet
had honest hearts. People in India to-day are divided
into higher classes, lower classes, or castes, and some are
looked upon as so low that the respectable classes will
not touch them. They are Untouchables.

Now, in Bengal (map), there are muddy places or marshes,
where crops will not grow because of the overmuch wet,
caused by the river rising in tides twice a day. What a
good change if the land could be drained and dried ! It
has often been done. Toiling men have made mats of
reeds and rushes, and piled them in piles on the ground.
The tides rise and carry mud into the meshes of the mats.
The tides fall, and flow towards the sea, and leave much
of the mud. Thus the mats collect earth, which increases
and makes so thick a layer that the soil rises above the
tide and dries ; and seeds may be sown, and trees planted,
and huts built, and people live in villages, and children
play, on land that once was marsh. A wonderful work,
indeed ; a great victory, indeed. And the people who have
done this wonder were Chandâlas, or Untouchables.

You see Baroda City on our map. I went there in 1913,
and visited a school where Untouchable girls and boys
were taught lessons, and were trained to be useful citizens.
Dark-skinned boys, with bare feet, wore pink turbans
and white jackets and dhotis (a little like knickers). At
the teacher's wish one of the lads sang, in a shrill voice,
while he lifted his eyes as if towards the heavens. He
sang a hymn. The words I knew not, for I was English,
and knew not his Hindu speech ; but I understood his
sparkling eyes, and the ring of his high voice. A friend
told me in a whisper that this hymn used never to be
sung by Untouchables ; it was forbidden to their lips.
But the Prince, or Maharajah, of Baroda, had said that the

[1] Tennyson's " Akbar's Dream."

Untouchables should sing this hymn, to show that they
were no longer considered vulgar and low, and thus the
poor and humble were lifted up.

Only the Rama story would be recited to younger children.
This lesson offers a complex of geography, literature, biography,
and even (if the ambitious term may pass) sociology. It is,
fundamentally, a history sketch, giving, in chronological order,
glimpses of the Indian Early Age, the Mogul Empire, and (in a
final anecdote that is more significant than may, at first sight,
appear) recent developments.

II. LESSON ON IRELAND

(THE MAP, WHEN COMPLETED, WILL SHOW IN OUTLINE,
IRELAND, CANTYRE, WEST COAST OF ENGLAND AND
WALES, FRANCE)

There was a king named Lir (*Lear*), who lived in the
" Never " time. His dear wife died, leaving him to look
after their four children—a girl, the eldest, and three boys.
King Lir cried bitterly as he bent over his sleeping children.
A while after he married a chief's daughter, but she, the
stepmother, hated the four children. One day, indeed,
she drew a sword to slay them, but she did not dare.
Another day, she put them in her chariot, and drove to
the waterside at Lough, or Lake, Derg (*draw a little lake*),
where the stream of Shannon (*map*) runs in and out again.
She sent them into the lake to paddle and bathe, and
shouted :
" Now you shall be birds ! "
The girl, Fionnuala, cried, " Stepmother ! you are a
witch ; have some pity on us. Do not let us be birds for
ever."
" Very well," the witch said, " you shall be birds till
the Woman from the South and the Man from the North
come together. Three hundred years you will stay here ;
then three hundred years at cold and stormy Cantyre ;

and three hundred years by the Western Sea and Eagle (Achill) island. (*Map.*) I will let you sing and you shall talk the Irish tongue."

King Lir searched far and wide for his lost darlings; and when he came to the lake, he heard his children calling, but he only saw four swans on the water. They told him they were his daughter and three sons, fated to be birds for nine hundred years; and he went home in great grief. As to the stepmother, the people hated her cruel act, and somebody touched her with a magic Druid wand and she became a spirit of the air, and wandered to the clouds, and perhaps she is there still! Folk came from all parts to hear the lovely songs of the four birds. " For there never was any music, nor any delight, heard in Ireland to compare with the music of the swans." They were on the lake—where the Shannon runs in and out—three hundred years. After that they flew to the hard rocks of Cantyre, where icy waves broke over them; and sometimes it was so cold that Fionnuala cuddled one brother to her feathery breast and a brother under each of her wings, and the wintry blast blew the snow over them. They stayed there three hundred years.[1] After that they went over to Connaught (*map*), and swam about Achill Island, till nine hundred years in all had passed. Then they flew to the house of their father Lir, and found it in ruins, and nobody lived there, and grass grew on the floor, and a cold kettle stood on the cold hearth; and the four birds sang their sweet song all night, very sad. " For there never was any music, nor any delight, heard in Ireland to compare with the music of the swans." At that time, an Irish woman from the South became queen to the Man in the North, that is, the King of Connaught. So then. . . .

But here I must break off awhile, and I will finish about the swans presently. Let us go across to Wales (*map*) and see how the robbers—the pirates—caused such terror to the country people. With yells the wild Irish pirates leaped from their boats and terrified the quiet cottagers and

---

[1] Primitive tale-makers, like children, played very loosely with numbers, a fact on the significance of which I have already dwelt in the remarks on mathematics.

labourers. Britons they were in that part; and the Romans, with their road-making, camp-building, and helmeted troops, had given peace and safety to Wales for long years; but times were troubled now. A sixteen-year-old lad, named Patrick, was dragged away with other captives, and they were carried oversea and sold as slaves. For six years Patrick was slave in the west to the King of Connaught, and he minded pigs and sheep on the green hills; and oft he knelt on the wet earth, or in the snow, and prayed.

One night an angel bade him go to the east and sail in a ship to his Fatherland. So he ran away, and tramped over bog and mire, to the eastern shore, even to Wicklow, where a ship lay in harbour. The ship carried a lot of hunting-dogs, good for pursuing game, and loud was their barking. When Patrick begged with tears and lifted hands, the ship-master let him take passage. But the ship did not sail straight to Wales. It voyaged to Gaul (*mark France*), where the company landed on a very wild shore, and they marched over wastes and ran short of water and food. Joyfully they met a herd of wild boars, some of which they killed, and the travellers had a feast of pork. No marvel was it that, after such a meal, Patrick dreamed a large rock rolled down a hill upon his stomach! They marched on, and Patrick, parted from the others, came to a pleasant island on the south coast (*map*) where monks prayed and sang psalms and trained vines, and Patrick joined their company. After that, he took a long journey home to his British parents, and rested a time. In a dream he saw an Irishman beckoning across the waters and saying, " We pray thee, holy youth, come again, and walk among us as before."

At last Patrick was a bishop, and he and his monks sailed to Ireland, and landed. A chief, sword in hand, came as if to kill, but, on hearing Patrick's good words, he behaved friendly and gave the strangers a cattle-shed to use as a Christian church.

Now, when the weather was warming in the spring at Easter, the Irish would light great bonfires, or set light to a man of straw, wood, and dry leaves, and only the King's

4

hand might kindle the fire at the Hill of Tara (*map*).
The King was angry when he saw a fire blaze ten miles
from Tara, and he and his nobles rode swiftly on horses
till they found Patrick standing by a fire that he had lit
for Easter.   He talked of Jesus who died on the Cross,
and of God, and then he plucked a green three-lobed
shamrock.

" Here," said he, " you see three parts in one leaf ; and
I have come to tell you Irish of the three Holy Ones—God
the Father, God the Son, and God the Holy Spirit."

After that he went to see Connaught, where he had
knelt once in the snow.   And he went to see the Pope of
Rome (*map*).   When back in Ireland he met a friendly
king at Armagh (*map*), where the monks were allowed to
build wood huts at the bottom of the hill.   One day,
on the hill top, Patrick saw a mother-deer and her little
fawn, nor would he let his comrades chase and kill the
wild creatures, for, on this spot, he desired a church to be
built, and there is a church there to this day.

His time of death drew near.   Sickness came upon him
and he died, and was buried near the church of the cattle-
shed, and angels sang at his funeral.   We remember his
death, and some of us wear the " dear little shamrock "
on St. Patrick's Day, March 17.   He died in the year 471.
A curious square bell was his, and people tell me you can
see this old clapper in a museum in Dublin to-day.[1]

After Patrick's death, a monk went about ringing this
bell to call folk to hear the Gospel.   One day, four swans
heard the bell and came to him, and he let them dwell
in a church by the altar.   The Queen of Connaught much
wanted to have these wonderful singing swans that could
understand sermons, and her husband went to the church
and laid rough hands upon the birds to capture them.
Lo ! their feathers all fell off, and people saw one very old
dame and three very old men—Fionnuala and her three
brothers, the children of Lir.   They asked the monk to
baptize them with water, and he did so, and then the four
Christians died and were buried under a stone that had

---

[1] For details of biography, see Prof. J. B. Bury's " Life of
St. Patrick " (1905).

strange Ogam writing on it. 'Tis an old style of talk, this Ogam. A scrap of it is heard in a song which school-children may sing :

> " Now is the month of may-ing,
> When merry lads are playing,
> Fal la la ! "

This " Fa la la ! " is Ogam talk, meaning, " All hail this day ! O joyful day ! "[1]

There was once a slave-woman in Connaught, who had a daughter born at sunrise on the first day of the spring season, and the angels called the girl Arrow of Fire, or Brigit. She was the first to weave a piece of cloth in Ireland. She minded cows and sheep, was a friend to birds, and fed poor folk ; and rich was the butter she made from milk. When she blessed the hands of harpers, their music sounded more lovely. She lived under an oak at Kildare (*map*) and was a friend of St. Patrick. Right in the midst of noisy London is a quiet church that bears her name—St. Bride, or St. Brigit.[2]

People call Ireland the Isle of Saints. You have heard of the saints' preaching and church-building, and bells, and feeding of the poor, and music, and butter-making. And there are folk in Ireland to-day who do things that are wonderful ; for all the wonders were not done in days of old. What would Brigit think if she could see, in the green Irish pastures, the farms and dairies and stores in which people join hands in farming, helping one another in their work, their buying and selling, their saving and spending, their butter trade, their bacon trade, their poultry trade, their egg trade, their cream trade. Oh, surely, she would bless the hands of the folk that play this music of labour and agriculture ! A wonder-man that helped this new Irish adventure was an Irishman who, for years,

---

[1] The full story of the Children of Lir will be found in Lady Gregory's delightful volume, " Gods and Fighting Men."

Obviously, the close of the story is a Christian addition to a pre-Christian legend.

[2] Lady Gregory's " Book of Saints " ; also Frazer's " Golden Bough."

farmed a ranch in America, and as he watched the fine tilling of the earth in that Western land, he dreamed— for why should not others besides St. Patrick dream ? He dreamed of this plan of joining together in agriculture ; he dreamed of Co-operation. So he crossed the seas home, and persuaded the people, and they answered him in right good will, and, by the year 1912, there were in Ireland a thousand Co-operative Societies. The man was Horace Plunkett.

Arrow of fire—Co-operation—speed on, and touch the hearts of the people, Irish and all !

What is the " subject " of this lesson ? Is it geography ? No, but it contains much geography, learned incidentally. Is it literature ? No, yet its literary connexions are many. Is it religion ? No, but I trust a certain whisper of the religious mind is heard. Is it economics ? No, yet its climax is a sort of naïve beautification of social economics. It is a history lesson.

It is once more understood that portions only of this talk are suited to younger pupils.

III. THE RIVER RHONE

(THE PRINCIPLE OF THE GROWING MAP BEING ESTABLISHED, PARENTHETICAL NOTES AS TO THE MAP CAN NOW BE DROPPED)

Our feet stand deep in the snow on the high mountains. Let us climb down, careful lest we slip. At the top there are no trees. As we go we arrive at forests of pine trees. Yet lower the air is warmer, and red roses grow, and we see the green grass pastures in the valley, and a stream runs there.

Beware ! A roaring flood may dash, swelling this river Rhone and bearing us away. The snow melts on the hills, and makes the flood. The people, industrious like bees or ants, build up earth-heaps, or dykes, to fence off the flooding waters from their cottages and gardens.

Our Rhone—it is yours and mine while we talk of it !—
runs from the valley of the " Alpine mountains cold "
(Milton's phrase) into a broad, smooth lake—Leman or
Geneva. Here, on the shore, are found old black and
rotted beams of wood, which once were parts of the water-
houses, or pile-dwellings, of Early men long before the days
of us English, French, Swiss (for Geneva is in Switzerland),
or even the Romans and the Greeks. Here are also found
bones of dog, pig, ox, goat, sheep, horse, beaver, etc., and
the tools and weapons of stone—which were the oldest—
bronze—the next oldest—and iron; also pottery. (Date
about 3000 B.C.)

We pass the City of Geneva, where the wise men of the
League of Nations meet in their office, and think deeply
of the affairs of the globe, even as far as the isles of the
Pacific or the forests of the pygmies in mid-Africa. The
river runs blue in colour, and rapid as an arrow ; so our
English poet Byron spoke (in " Childe Harold ") of " the
blue rushing of the arrowy Rhone."

Danger ! The river dips into a dark, rocky tunnel.
About 1890, two men rowing in a boat were swept by the
strong current into this tunnel, and never seen again alive.
Farther down, the stream breaks from the tunnel into the
open valley.

Light, sparkling light ! You see lamps lighting villages
and towns at dusk. You hear the grind of machinery
sawing wood in saw mills built near the river. Whence
comes the power that kindles the light, and moves the
machines ? It is electric power, and this is created by the
water-power of the rushing Rhone. So the same river
that brought death to the two rowers may be mastered by
the mind of man, and made to give light, and to slave
for us in the mills.[1]

In the north of the Rhone valley lies a small town
(Lons-le-Saunier, not necessarily named here) where, one
evening, a young man, violin in hand, hummed and
strummed, walked up and down, hummed and strummed,

---

[1] I believe the term, " White coal " (*houille blanche*), was first
employed to denote water-power by a French engineer in the
Rhone region.

and made up a song, words and music. Not long after a band of citizens from Marseilles marched to Paris, carrying the red-white-and-blue flag, and singing the young man's song ; and it has since been known as the " Marseillaise." (*Have the tune played*.) The first words run, " Allons, enfants de la Patrie " — " Come, children of the Fatherland ! " It was the time of the great overturning, or French Revolution (1792).

Here is the city of silk-weavers, machines, and factories— Lyons. A bridge of four wide arches crosses the Rhone— Pont Wilson (Wilson Bridge). It was opened on July 14, 1918, when the American armies were helping us—the Allies, English and French—to beat back the Germans to their own country. The City of Lyons gave thanks to President Wilson by naming this bridge after him.

Hereabouts, in our valley, is an ancient city where a statue shows an armoured knight dying, and looking, as he dies, at the cross of his sword-handle, for he thinks of the cross of Christ. He never felt fear, and none reproached him for evil deeds ; and this horseman, or chevalier, was Bayard, the knight " without fear and without reproach." The city is Grenoble. When he was wounded, his men bore him to a house where dwelt a lady and her two daughters. The sick man spake most sternly to his soldiers that none should harm these three ladies ; and the elder lady gave him her best care till he was healed. As he mounted his horse to leave and return to the French army, the two girls brought him gifts which they had made—a pair of bracelets done in twisted gold and silver thread, and a purse of crimson silk ; and he said he would cherish these presents to the last. And this he did. Many were the mourners at his death by battle-wounds in 1524. Bayard's motto was, " Do thy duty, come what may."[1]

In this Rhone land, Romans were masters once. They, with their short swords and strong hands, had made Gaul (France) and Spain part of their Republic. They needed swords and strong hands to guard their Latin country when Hannibal and his fierce African hosts

[1] The full story of Bayard is given in my " Stories for Young Hearts and Minds."

marched from Spain across the Rhone at this City of Orange towards the Alpine mountains and Italy. At Orange we can still see the open space and the terrace of stone seats, and the place for the actors' stage, which formed the Roman theatre. Elsewhere we may view bridges of half-circle arches that carried water (aqueducts) from the lakes and hill-streams to the cities. A famous family was named after this City of Orange, and one of its princes was William of Orange, that is, William III, King of England. Here, also, there lived a man who would climb hills to study plants, or sit on the ground for hours, watching, through a glass lens, the ways of insects, spiders, and other living things.[1] He was Henri Fabre, and this man of nature-study died in 1915, aged ninety-two.

A shepherd lad, aged twelve, watched his flock in the pasture (twelfth century), when—so the tale goes—a voice from heaven called three times :

" Benezet, build a bridge over the Rhone at Avignon."

" I do not know the place," he said, " and I have no money but three pennies."

Then appeared a bearded pilgrim with a staff—it was an angel—who led him to the swift-running river.

" Cross," ordered the angel, " and go into the city and speak to the bishop."

Benezet saw a ferryman who agreed and took him over to Avignon, and the lad walked up the steep street into the cathedral where the bishop stood in a pulpit, preaching to the citizens.

" Sir," cried the shepherd boy, " Jesus Christ bids me build a bridge over the Rhone."

" Beadle," called the bishop, " take this boy to the magistrate to be chastised for shouting in the House of God."

" Boy," said the magistrate to Benezet, " I will believe you can build a bridge, and I will not chastise you, if you lift yoh stone and bear it to the river."

Benezet prayed, and then lifted a stone which thirty men could only just shake, and carried it to the bank of the stream ready to form part of the first arch. All the

---

[1] Anecdotes of Fabre are omitted for brevity's sake.

city was stirred. People gave money. Workmen came to labour, and the stone bridge was begun. It went on for years. The monk-pontiffs, or bridge-builders of that age could not build fast. Before the work was ended, the young pontiff died, and he—St. Benezet—was buried in a chapel on the middle of the bridge. There were nineteen arches in all, and the bridge lasted till 1679; and now only four broken arches remain to tell of the faith and industry of the folk of the Middle Ages.

In a valley near Avignon there are woods, and bees are many among the flowers; and a wonderful green fountain sparkles; and there are shady caves. A young Italian used to walk and brood under the oak trees and dream his poet's dreams. One day he went into a church in the city, and among the worshipping folk he beheld a lady with a most grave and sweet face, and her robe was green, sown with violets; and he loved her. Full of sorrow was he when this lady, Laura, died, and he—Petrarch, the poet—wrote verses of affection, in which he tells of her grace and goodness, and her passing to heaven; and, though his tears were shed so long ago (fourteenth century) many eyes to-day still read, and love to read, his noble verses.[1]

Now we approach the sea. We cross low and marshy plains. Here is the Mid-land or Mediterranean Sea. Before the Romans ruled the Rhone there came brave Greek seafarers in ships moved by sails and oars, and they built a city which we now call Marseilles, a busy port, with a crowd of vessels in the harbour. Visitors climb a hill to a church on the top of which a gilded Mary, "Notre-Dame de la Garde"—"Our Lady that Guards"—glistens in the sunshine. Even in the war time (1916) French labour began cutting a canal from Marseilles to the river Rhone at Arles city. Some day such a straight water-road may run all the way from the sea, along the Rhone valley to Geneva, and sea-going ships may anchor near the gate of the House of the League of Nations. Great are the French. *Vive la France* !—Long live France !

[1] Much of the material in this talk is gathered from Lenthéric's " Le Rhône, du Saint Gothard à la Mer " (1892).

The method of this Rhone lesson causes the talk to leap from age to age, backwards and forwards. We might close (in the case of pupils aged 12–14), by sorting our elements into ages, a process quite easy to children trained by our historical plan ; thus : (1) Time of Early man, and lake-dwellings. (2) Time of Greek sailors. (3) Time of Roman builders. (4) Time of Catholic, or Middle Age (St. Benezet). (5) Modern time of Petrarch, Bayard, William of Orange, Lyons silk factories, French Revolution, Marseilles docks, Fabre, Wilson Bridge, League of Nations. (6) Time of To-morrow, when the Geneva-Mediterranean canal will be completed. Thus, our kaleidoscope has mingled many themes in one historical synthesis—geography, biography, poetry, science, art, industry, love, and death.

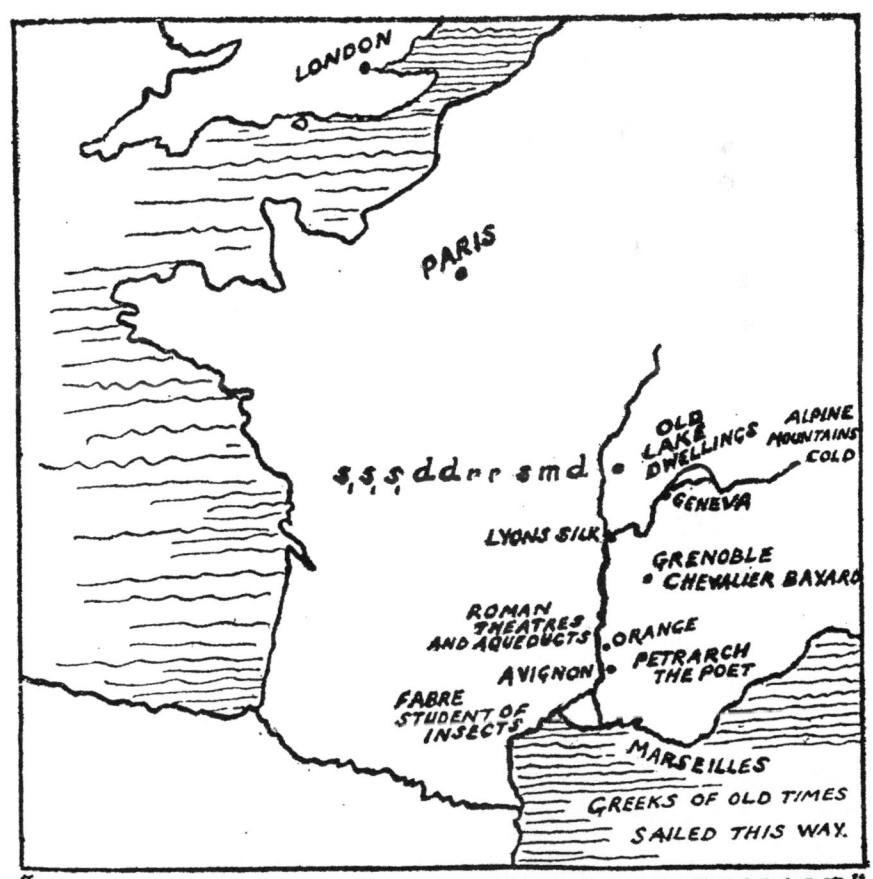

"BLUE RUSHING OF THE ARROWY RHONE."
(LORD BYRON).

These three lessons illustrate, in spirit rather than in precise form, a species of recapitulation. By such means pupils, aged fourteen or fifteen, may take backward glances along the ages through which the teacher has led them since the first simple adventures in history in the kindergarten.   For the age of fourteen or fifteen indeed, the type of language I have employed is too elementary.   But this simplicity has been a reminder that the process of historical thought opened when the school-child's career opened.

CHAPTER III

THE CATHOLIC-FEUDAL AGE

(TO ABOUT 1300)

WHEN the Gothic tribes plundered Rome in 410, Augustine sought consolation and peace in the thought of " one holy and united society, which we call the City of God."

> There we shall rest and see ; we shall see and love ; we shall love and praise. . . . For what other thing is our end, but to come to that Kingdom of which there is no end ?

His work on the " City of God " (completed in 426), however much it erred in its judgment on the value of Roman civilization, rightly and instinctively pointed to a new European period, which would be dominated by the Catholic faith. The opening of this Mediæval, or Catholic-feudal, stage is very justly dated from the days of St. Augustine. But we should guard against allowing the European term " Catholic-feudal " to screen our view from important historical developments in Asia and Africa.

In the Catholic-feudal Age, slavery evolved into the milder form of serfdom. Village-life and agriculture in western Europe rested on a more or less communal basis ; craft-guilds and merchant-guilds and municipal self-government unfolded together ; and the use of money began to displace barter in trade, and to modify serfage into wagedom. Such economic changes prepared the way for the modern rise of Labour in social and political life and institutions. The honour paid to Mary from the fifth century onwards, and culminating in the Lady-chapels of cathedrals and the heavenly Vision of Dante ; the impressive part played by women in the mediæval legends of saints and the growth of feminine elements in popular romances—foreshadowed the later Woman Movement. Europe was affected by a double evolution which, on one side, established a Catholic unity with all the spiritual and æsthetic influences represented by church, clergy, monastic orders, cathedral buildings, church music and dramatic activities, schools and universities ; and, on the other side, created nationalities (England, France, Hungary, and the rest) which co-operated with the Catholic power, or conflicted with it, and (England leading) evolved Parliamentary institutions. The social spirit took on new and remarkable forms. It expressed itself in the devoted monks, nuns, saints, and missionaries who were the precursors of the later types of civic and philanthropic servants. It linked up scattered communities, through pilgrimages, on a wide scale. It flung itself into a test, which was moral as well as material, with the Mohammedan power in the Crusades. Despite gross cruelties and perversions (as in the Crusades also), its attempt, through the Inquisition, was to establish an absolute moral and religious standard ; an attempt which, happily, failed, and yet was, at heart, not meanly motived. It sent merchants and explorers to unmapped coasts and wildernesses, and so blazed the trail for the Age of Expansion, 1300–1914.

To teachers who, led by misinterpretations of history and psychology, have been trained to class this noble period as the Dark Ages, I have nothing to offer. I suppose they must either omit it altogether, or rush through it at break-neck speed in order to shorten their distress, or else maintain one long incantation of cursing. This last method is the worst, since negativism is a dissolving agent in education, both injuring the mind of the learner, and destroying the delicacy of the teaching instrument.

We will glance at the economic side of Catholic-feudal life, noting the plants, animals, minerals, and industries which will afford abundant concrete objects of study ; and then briefly review the religious, literary, and political sides ; all the time expanding our map, which will now stretch to Ireland on the west, and China on the east, and take us again (in connexion with the religion of Islam) to Arabia. Reading and writing should be largely associated with the topics of the period, and arithmetic (still kept simple and concrete) will borrow natural themes from the money and weights and measures which evolved many characteristic forms in the age now under consideration. Certain repetitions of subjects from the Early Age will occur, for example, wool re-appears in our catalogue of animal products. In the Middle Ages, wool assumed immense importance, and not least in England ; and illustrated lessons on wool should on no account be omitted. And the allusion just made to England reminds us that, in the Catholic-feudal period, the rise of English nationality constitutes a vital theme.

Among plant products we note : Cotton, muslin (from Mosul), gauze (from Gaza), flax, with its associated spinning-wheel and many a fairy-tale, diaper (from Ypres—*d'Ypres*), damask (from Damascus), saffron (grown in the fifteenth century at Saffron Walden), sugar, pepper, cloves, ginger, cinnamon, cummin-seed, mustard, nuts, lemon, apricot, melon, almonds, vinegar, wine, hops, ale, figs, raisins, rice, beans, peas, rye (a staple food of peasants) onions, leek (in Wales), parsnips, cauliflower, carrots, beech-tree yieldings wine's food. The orange arrives commercially in the fourteenth century.

Animal products : Cattle, cheese, swine, sheep—

" It is not for nothing that the Lord Chancellor of to-day sits on a woolsack. . . . The profits from wool and woollen manufactures was the cause of the wars which the historian puts down to all sorts of constitutional, personal, and ecclesiastical causes. . . . The supply of wool had been for centuries almost a monoply of England. . . . We find payments to the King's Exchequer from guilds of weavers at London, Lincoln, and Oxford. . . . We have notices of them at Winchester, Nottingham, and Huntingdon.   The kings encouraged the formation of guilds of weavers, granting them privileges, and using them to organize and control trade. . . . As early as 1157 the people of Cologne had a Hanse and Guildhall in England ; other towns joined them ; Lübeck began the great Hanseatic League.   Cloth was the basis of all ; it continued until a very late date to be the money of such places as the Orkney and Shetland Islands." J. W. Jeudwine's " Foundations of Society " (1918). About eighty-five German cities formed the League, which traded eastwards in Russia, westwards in England, and governed the Baltic commerce.

Sturgeon, herring (then a very important article of food), whalebone and oil, ivory from Asia, furs, skins, silk, honey. A reference to the Black Rat may almost seem trifling ; but this rat was brought from the East in the Crusaders' ships, and spread the plague which had such immense results in the social life of Europe.[1]

Minerals : Copper, tin, lead, iron (armour), salt, alum (turkey-red dye).

In addition to manufactures already alluded to, we may name tapestry, Venetian glass, and paper from woollen rags. The increased use of woollen shirts, which accompanied rising prosperity, led to a larger supply of rags, and the paper thus manufactured greatly facilitated the progress of the printing-press soon after the close of the Middle Ages.

Among buildings are to be remarked bridges, manor-houses, guildhalls, and castles. The castle figures in history and legend mainly as a fortress ; but it should be remembered that it often served as a place of refuge, and a food-store against famine, for the inhabitants of protected villages.

It would be worth the while of an ingenious teacher, assisted by the children, to frame a rough model of a feudal village, with its manor-house, church, farm-houses, cottages, strips of open field without hedges, hay-meadows, village green, and the common or waste land around, the royal forest, and a baron's castle in the margin. It would be needless to burden young pupils with rigid accounts of the communal farming ; but, at least, they can understand how the husbandmen changed their land-strips from time to time, and used ploughs and tools that belonged to the village. The unfenced common-land was used by the villagers' cattle and swine, and any villager might here capture fish, birds, and wild quadrupeds ; while the kings

[1] M. A. C. Hinton's "Rats and Mice, the Enemies of Mankind " (1918).

preserved the enclosed forests, with their valuable timber and game. Enclosures and hedges, and individual ownership came later, but, at one time, a third part of England consisted of wastes and commons on which the people's rights of pasture, hunting, etc., were guarded by feudal law ; though much of the rural custom had been inherited from old English days before the Norman Conquest. Many surnames remain to-day as reminders of village labour and craft : smith, carpenter, carter, miller, thatcher, hayward, woodward, cow-herd (coward), shepherd, pinder (cattle-impounder), bailey (steward), and the like. As to the forests, ballads and legends will furnish ample romance, though it is as well to bear in mind Mr. Jeudwine's stern comment on

" The irresponsible poachers—the Robin Hoods, Little Johns, and Maid Marians—who had little or no land or cattle of their own, and made their living in the waste land, destroying the food supply, burning the timber, watching on the edge of the woods for the animals which they were driving in the open, and disturbing and driving on to cultivated land vermin and beasts of prey."[1]

Not a few fairy tales hint at the awe felt by people of the valley and plain for the vagabonds and uncouth tribesmen of the forests. Professor Fleure observes that

" There can be little doubt that the local (German) folk-lore, that collected by the Grimms, for instance, is related to the clearing of the forest, the clash of grass-landers and hill men and forest hunters, the finding of nests of wild aboriginal folk in the forest depths."[2]

[1] J. W. Jeudwine's " Foundations of Society and the Land " contains much valuable information on mediæval rural life.

[2] " Human Geography in Western Europe " (1918).

Town life should be richly presented by means of models and pictures, with such elementary comments as may rouse a sense of the beauty of certain old types of building, and help to lay a modest foundation for interest in modern town-planning. The subject of merchant-guilds (associations of traders) and of craft-guilds (associations of weavers, dyers, tanners, pewterers, goldsmiths, butchers, pepperers, grocers, tailors, skinners, girdlers, fletchers, etc.), is of great social and political importance. Material for lively description, or even simple play-acting, may be indicated : Processions between church and guildhall ; banquets ; choice of officers (tickets bearing names of candidates drawn from a box by a child or priest) ; journeymen's oaths by gospels and saints to be loyal to masters ; apprentices' oaths, and masters' vow to care for apprentices in sickness or health ; craft and market rules ; how many times cloth should be dipped in dye ; colour and size of garments ; bad fish not to be sold, nor stale meat, nor rotten eggs, nor sham jewellery ; guilds constructed roads, canals, harbours, halls, fountains, hospitals, promenades, churches, belfries.[1]

One could wish that, for school use, copies could be multiplied of the charming stained-glass pictures in Chartres Cathedral (thirteenth century) of more than fifty local trades in action. There had, of course, been artisan guilds and benefit clubs in ancient Rome ; but the mediæval guilds greatly contributed to experience in self-government, economic and municipal, and to national evolution.

" All the fun of the fair," with jesters, conjurors, and stalls should be pictured :

[1] See G. Renard's " Guilds in the Middle Ages," trans. Intro. by G. D. H. Cole.

5

The Romans held wool and cloth fairs at Winchester. In the Middle Ages, in fair-time, all shops within seven miles of the city of Winchester were closed. Tolls were exacted at entrances by road or bridge. The great common was divided into temporary streets for drapery, spicery, pottery, etc. (Compare the scenes of Vanity Fair in Bunyan's " Pilgrim's Progress.")

Trade routes have their dramatic aspects : transport by oxen, mules, horses, by caravans of camels ; by Venetian ships, or huge Flanders galleys propelled by 180 oarsmen and guarded against pirates by bands of archers ;[1] and, if pictures are available, something may be told of the travels of the Venetian, Marco Polo, over Asiastic deserts to China, India, Sumatra, etc., and of his dictating, in a Genoese prison, the story of his twenty-six years of wandering (1269 to 1295).

At this point enters money, as a tremendous factor in modern civilization. Trade had largely been barter ; labour had been rendered for maintenance, and rents paid in kind. Gold coin, scarcely known since the seventh century, was revived in the gold florin (of Florence) ; and mediæval coins had chiefly been silver. Twenty of the silver *solidus* coins made a pound-weight, or *libra*, and twelve *deniers* made a *solidus*, or shilling, coins being represented by the letters £ s. d. Money, indeed, helped to close the Catholic-feudal phase ; the ease of money-transaction carried trade far beyond local markets and guilds, and the labour of money-wage-earners was found to be more manageable and profitable than serf-labour. The use of money in trade gave birth to the social Middle Class of western Europe. In this class began to appear the rich and serious citizens who built new parish churches, and grammar-schools, such as the school at Chipping Campden. At

[1] See Clive Day's " History of Commerce " (1907).

Chipping Campden there is a famous brass memorial to William Grevil, " the flower of the wool-merchants of all England." Speaking of the effigies on the tombs of such citizens, Mr. R. H. Gretton remarks :

> " The first men to hand themselves down to posterity, not in mail armour or plate armour and heraldic surcoats, but frankly in the plain fur gown of the civilian, with an inkhorn in place of a sword, or a sheep and a woolpack at the feet instead of a lion, must have been very proud of their position, very self-confident, and perhaps not a little self-assertive. Their brasses at least convey to us how securely the Middle Class was establishing itself in the State." " The English Middle Class " (1917).

The glories of the architecture of the Middle Ages should be known to all young people through coloured prints—domes, spires, arches, columns, buttresses— the porphyry pillars and Byzantine mosaics of St. Sophia, as well as the carvings of Durham Cathedral. The pictures in the twelfth century stained glass should be familiar, and the melodies of chiming bells repeated on the piano or in song. Do not forget to recite a story of whole populations co-operating to build a church, as at St. Denis, Paris, when rich folk harnessed themselves to carts loaded with stones. In this historic Catholic atmosphere may be retold the Bible stories, not as vehicles of doctrine (with which the present work has no relation), but as interpretations of the windows and carvings of churches, and the festivals and worship of villagers, serfs, lords of the manor, Crusaders, monks, guildsmen, merchants, and the gossips and loiterers by the market cross or wayside well. I have already advised that the Bible stories and parables should be unfolded when the teacher unfolds the drama of their age of origin and acceptance—that is, up to the year A.D. 400. But it was Catholic Europe which, in its institutions and literature, absorbed the Christian and Hebrew tradition with a new and peculiar enthusiasm, and, if one may so speak, reorganized the whole of the vast Biblical epic, and re-fashioned it for the people's eye and ear. In this world of the chancel, nave, aisle, organ, and cloister, girt about with the green lawns of the cathedral close, should the stately scenes of patriarchal and gospel life be re-enacted, and not through the dismal method of catechisms, manuals, and examinations ?[1] In the same spirit one may narrate such episodes of the Lives of the Saints as are suited to the children's capacity. Take this stray instance :

An old moralist relates that " a bird flying in the fields was pursued by a hawk. She saw him coming, and, as she had been taught at home, began to cry, ' Holy Thomas, save me ! ' and at once the hawk fell down dead, and the bird escaped unhurt. Lo, sirs ! What virtue it is to call on Saint Thomas of Canterbury in any tribulation." G. G. Coulton's " Social Life in Britain " (1918).

Such an anecdote, appended to a recital of the death of Thomas à Becket, really explains itself as a form of hero-worship. If asked critical questions, the teacher will, of course, reply that this is but a legend. It is, however, an error to suppose that children, intelligently trained, will need a specific argumentation every time a legend is told. If history is consistently taught them for inspiration, they will, aided by a judicious hint from time to time, distinguish without laboured discussion, between the obvious legend and the

[1] The inspiration of religious poetry has been marred by those dull, scholastic devices, just as the glory of human logic has been spoiled by deadly systems of arithmetical " sums."

normal actuality, and, in either case, appreciate the message. It is precisely thus that they are able to admire the immortal poetry of the Greeks.

Among typical saints may be named St. Benedict, St. Genevieve (the shepherdess of Paris), St. Columba (the Irish missionary to Iona), St. Francis of Assisi, St. Isidore (the Spanish ploughman), St. Bernard of Clairvaux, St. Elizabeth of Hungary; and certain legends of " Our Lady " should be included.[1] An excellent example is St. Benedict, whose life is here summarized in highly abridged notes :

B, as a young man, lived in a cave near Rome, his food (signalled by bell), being let down in a basket from cliff above, by Brother Romanus, who occupied a similar cave.   Goatherds and shepherds climbed up to hear B's preaching.   Others joined, and B's band of " monks " built twelve little houses in valley, chanted psalms, did daily labour.   At Monte Cassino, B flung down image of Apollo, God of Sunshine and Health, raised the Cross, founded monastery, and a Rule : " Idleness is the enemy of the soul, and therefore, at fixed times, the brothers ought to be occupied in manual labour ; and again, at fixed times, in sacred reading."   To a man who said he wished to leave the evil world, B replied " Go and work," giving him a bill-hook to clear briars.   A King of Goths visited, bowed low to B, who sat among black-robed monks, listened to counsel, and henceforward behaved more mercifully in war.   B and sister met yearly on hill-side, talking of holy things.   Both buried in same grave (543).   Benedictines tilled, felled, planted, hived bees, bred cattle, made roads, gardened, constructed bridges, fed poor, grew medical herbs, taught in cloister-schools, copied manuscripts, painted missal illuminations, built splendid abbeys. Benedictine nuns worked vestments, and lace at Valenciennes. St. Boniface of Devonshire was a B.   So also St. Dunstan, who was mason, carpenter, smith, painter, designer, singer, music composer, musical-instrument maker.

[1] Mr. Victor Branford's admirable " St. Columba : a Study of Social Inheritance and Spiritual Development " should be consulted.   Baring-Gould's " Lives of the Saints " (15 vols.), gives ample details, and yet fuller material is contained in the " Bollandists."   A classical work is Montalembert's " Monks of the West."

In the sphere of music, we cannot do better than follow the guidance of Baring-Gould's and Cecil J. Sharp's "English Folk-Songs for Schools," and note how readily the themes harmonize with the life traced in our previous pages : "Shepherds," "Flowers in the Valley," "Morning Dew," "Poor Old Horse," "Huntsman," "Haymakers," "Strawberry Fair," "Farmer's Song," "Jolly Waggoner," "The Miller," "Dark-eyed Sailor," "Coasts of Barbary" (pirates), "Wars in High Germany" (with a sort of mystical geography), "Knights," "Magicians." A glimpse of the Troubadours of Provence should be entertaining ; as also an account of games : chess, blindman's buff, skittles, hot cockles (kneeling player guesses who strikes his hands outstretched behind), etc. Thus we naturally arrive at the drama, if one may use the term in its natural significance, and without thinking of the theatres, which were only established after the Catholic-feudal Age. Here is a dramatic suggestion from a page of A. W. Pollard's "English Miracle Plays" :

St. Francis of Assisi, at his altar in the forest, represented the Nativity scene with a real child, real men, and women, a real ox and ass. At any primitive little Italian town, when the members of the different religious guilds and fraternities walk in procession on Corpus Christi Day, little children toddle among them, dressed some with a tiny sheepskin and staff to represent John the Baptist, others in sackcloth as St. Mary Magdalen, others in a blue robe, with a little crown, as the Blessed Virgin, others again with an aureole tied to their little heads, as the Infant Saviour.

In Winchester Cathedral, dialogues with action represented the Holy Sepulchre, the Angels, and the Women; and bells chimed at the Resurrection.[1] Another

---

[1] Churches had no pews in those times.

religious enthusiasm, far removed from the dreary system of catechism and doctrinal handbook, was manifested in the Mediæval Pilgrimage, of which Chaucer, in the fourteenth century, was to render so vivid a chronicle. As in the case of the Canterbury Pilgrims, so also in the famous Summer Pilgrimages to the church of St. James in the Field of the Star (Santiago da Compostella) in Spain, long remembered by the children's grottos enshrining lighted candles, these wanderings were social tours, and had even commercial aspects, as well as fulfilling vows of piety. By way of contrast, and if it is not too sad a tale to tell, one might relate the legend of Ahasuerus, the Wandering Jew, who typified an ancient and noble race that, amid the rising nationalities of Europe, found no settled resting-place. Various admirable parables from ths Talmud should display the moral life of the Jewish people.[1]

In the view of the philosophic historian, the Crusades represent a conflict of two great monotheisms and civilizations (Catholic and Moslem), a very significant military European " League of Nations," and an economic drive of Europe (and particularly the Venetian Republic) towards the East. These themes are not for children, but they are at the base of the teacher's thought. The stories of Peter the Hermit, Godfrey, Richard, Saint Louis, can be so recited as to bring out the elements of devotion and co-operation ; and, at a later stage, the romantic poem of Tasso's " Jerusalem Delivered " may be given in outline. On the other hand, now is the opportunity for sympathetic sketches

---

[1] Selections by Polano or Hershon ; and many stories are scattered through the volumes of the " Jewish Encyclopædia."

of the career of Mohammed, and for introducing the more serious aspects of Arabian and Moorish biography, or, on the lighter side, the " Arabian Nights' Entertainments " ; with liberal assistance from pictures of Moslem life, manners, architecture, etc., both mediæval and later.[1] The economic aspect has been indicated, in a concrete way, in our list of plant, animal, and mineral products, and of manufactured articles. Such topics carry us, without difficulty, to India and its increasing trade with Europe ; and yet farther to China, and its contributions, namely, compasses, printing-blocks, silk, porcelain, glass lenses, cotton-weaving, coal-fuel, gunpowder, firearms, playing-cards, etc. Here is a silk legend :

An Indian prince, named Hate-Rain, married a Chinese princess, named Hate-Sun, and they had a fair daughter, named Girl-with-Golden-Hair. The mother died, the King married again, and the stepdaughter's life was made a misery, and yet she rose triumphant out of every affliction. Poor Goldilocks was exposed to lions, and (like Spenser's Una) rode home on one of those obliging beasts. Cast out into a wilderness, she was fed by vultures, found by one of the King's courtiers, and brought to the palace. Left on a desert island, she was rescued in a fisherman's boat. When she was buried in the earth of the royal courtyard, golden rays shot up and astonished the King, who had the spot dug up, and out came Golden Hair. Then the King packed her in a hollow mulberry tree trunk. She floated to Japan, and died in the arms of a Japanese on the seashore. Now, Golden Hair was the cocoon of yellow milk, which first China, then India, and then Japan utilized for manufacture ; and it is said that Japanese silk-growers still denote four phases in the life of the silk-worm by terms borrowed from the foregoing myth—Lion, Vulture, Boat, and Court. Adapted from J. B. Giraud's " Les Origines de la Soie " (1883).

[1] It is impossible to provide illustrative stories in this concise chapter. A considerable number of Moslem stories, such as that of the noble Antar the Black, occur in my " Youth's Noble Path " (Pub., Longmans) ; and the legend of Mohammed's flight to Paradise is given in my " Conduct Stories."

We turn next to schools and universities. The schools were, of course, monastic, and chiefly intended to train clergy. Modern children might be interested in a scrap of the " Colloquy," written by a Dorsetshire abbot, Ælfric, in the tenth century, especially if the teacher prepares the way by a reminder of the important place once, and still, held by Latin.[1] A master forms a new class out of a mixed group, who politely beg him to instruct them in talking good Latin.

> *Master :* " Are you willing to be flogged ? "
> *Boys :* " Yes, if you don't do it too much ! "
> *Master :* " What are you, and what do you do ? "
> *Various boys :* " Young monk," " ploughboy," " shepherd,"
> " cowherd," " hunter," " fisherman," " hawker," " merchant,"
> " seaman," " shoemaker," " salter," " cook," " baker."
> The master promises to supply Latin terms to fit the objects and activities of their employments, and each recites a list. The merchant, for example, enumerates goods bought from over-sea—purple, silk, gems, gold, wine, oil, ivory, brass, tin, sulphur, glass, and so on. And the chat closes with the reflection that each person should offer his best service in his particular field of labour. Mr. A. F. Leach quotes the " Colloquy " in his " Schools of Mediæval England," (1915).

Only very faint notions of a university can be given to girls and boys ; but they can at least go so far as to learn that, at the close of the Catholic-feudal time, teachers (" doctors ") would talk to young fellows who sat on straw-covered floors, in Paris, Bologna, Oxford, or Cambridge, and give lessons in right ways of speaking and arguing, and in arithmetic, geometry, astronomy, and music. Thus, without the children being burdened with the terms " Trivium " and " Quadrivium," they

---

[1] Children have often told me they knew no Latin, and I have amused myself and them by showing how many terms in daily use are really Latin. " Go home," I have said, " and tell your parents what a heap of Latin you know ! "

have caught the general idea of mediæval education (grammar, rhetoric, logic, arithmetic, etc.). And if our school walls were richly and rightly adorned, we might even show children coloured copies of the symbolic figures of these " Sacred Seven," as frescoed in the Church of Santa Maria Novella at Florence. But, perchance, imagination here becomes too daring !

Science, in the modern sense, was inactive in this period, and our children, without much hint from the Middle Ages, may continue their simple but progressive exercises in observation, experiment, measuring, etc. In arithmetic they will note the mediæval coinage already referred to, and pick up a not-altogether-trivial lesson when comparing twentieth-century prices with those operating when wage-earning commenced, e.g., a penny would buy a chicken, or four pounds of bread ; two pennies a fowl ; three, a goose. Our measures of capacity seem to be mediæval, and perhaps also the use of a rumbling ton (*tonneau*, the thunderous cask) for the carriage of wine. The name of Roger Bacon should be recorded, if only by the aid of the popular legend of the talking brass head which he constructed ; but a simple note of his laborious study, and his Oxford teaching (illustrated by a photograph of the fine statue of him now in Oxford) might be possible. The Catholic period was too occupied with great moral, social, and political issues to have leisure for " science " ; yet, in many respects, it cultivated the keenest intellectual power. The profound reflections of Dante on human sin and virtue, suffering and hope, are adequate proof. I am inclined to think, indeed, that a careful selection of pictures illustrating the " Divine Comedy " (such as the milder and more benign of Doré's), with elementary comments, would leave healthy impressions, much healthier than many melodramas of the kinema palace. To the literary materials, already mentioned, we may add selected Norse tales, the Arthur legends, the Nibelungs' Treasure legend,[1] and the charming Celtic tales in the Welsh " Mabinogion." [2]

Mr. J. W. Jeudwine, in his caustic way, says " we want a new elementary history of the British Islands which can forget that there was ever such a thing as a Parliament." I so far agree that, in the present scheme, I have placed economics, religious life, and literature before any reference to the Parliament, which, as a political expression, was compelled into existence by the social and intellectual pressure of an evolving nation. The rise of our Parliament in the thirteenth century must certainly be noted and impressed ; but children should on no account be laden with details of legislation. It will suffice to tell them that our growing England, like a growing child, needed increased money for maintenance, and that the barons, knights, burgesses, and priests who threaded their way on horseback or mule from hill and moor, village and castle, town and manor,

---

[1] Told in full in my " Stories for Moral Instruction."

[2] " In the centre of the chamber King Arthur sat upon a seat of green rushes, over which was spread a covering of flame-coloured satin, and a cushion of red satin was under his elbow. Then Arthur spoke : ' If I thought you would not disparage me,' said he, ' I would sleep while I wait for my repast ; and you can entertain one another with relating tales, and can obtain a flagon of mead and some meat from Kai.' And the King went to sleep. . . ."
This opening of the twelfth century pretty legend of " The Lady of the Fountain," is quoted to show the style. (See Lady Guest's translation of the Mabinogion, in Dent's " Everyman's Library.")

to Winchester or Westminster, were chiefly occupied, at first, with methods of taxation. Nor should the growth of other nationalities and Parliaments be forgotten. For example, one might relate the story of the Swiss mountaineers (not excluding the Tell legend), and perhaps show a picture of a modern Cantonal open-air Parliament, precisely democratic in the sense that every citizen is asked to attend.[1]

In addition to the events already alluded to in broad outlines, I do not think children at this stage (of ages about 10 to 12) need hear of more than the life of Alfred, the general meaning of the Norman Conquest, and the wars with France. The old-fashioned, dreary plodding through royal " reigns," dated in mechanical slices, was as ineffective and even injurious as the old-fashioned torture of " sums."

Whether in referring to the French wars, or other tumultuous episodes, tragic aspects of history necessarily reveal themselves. Care should, therefore, be taken to lighten the scene by telling of efforts of peace-makers. For example :

" In the south of France, where the Pyrenees mountains lift their jagged peaks, a Council of Catholic priests was held in the year 1027. The Council passed a resolution, calling on all Christian barons who felt they must needs fight, to mind at least certain good rules, to wit : Never to hurt women, or priests, or labourers tilling the soil, or travellers who journeyed peaceably on business ; and to observe a quiet time, or Truce of God, from any Wednesday evening to the next Monday morning ; and not to shed blood on such holy days as Easter and Christmas, or at the sacred season of the Lent Fasting. For about 200 years some barons in some places and at some times kept the Truce in France and other European lands ; and then came the age of bigger armies, which marched long distances and used cannon ; and the old Truce custom dropped. But honour be to the noble

[1] See an interesting photo on p. 1309 of Hutchinson's " History of the Nations."

Frenchmen who first set the custom going, and lit the signal-lamp of self-control." Quoted from my booklet "Towards a World at Peace" (1919).

For modelling, drawing, or colouring the following subjects may be named : castles, churches, city walls and gates, manor houses, barns, market crosses, wind-mills, bells, royal seals, city seals, crozier, armour, heraldic patterns (in colour), weapons, drums, tankards, horn lanterns, jester's cap and bells, viking and other ships, etc.[1] And some children may like to amuse themselves with drawing maps in the mediæval manner, with fishes and boats on the sea, and castles, etc., on land.[2]

Students of Dr. Hayward's scheme of "School Celebrations," in which pictures, busts, pageantry, music, recitation of choice prose and verse, and memorial praise of the servants of humanity are blended in many-toned and many-coloured festival, will discover, in this Catholic-feudal Age, innumerable suggestions for a variety of such ceremonials. There is an ample field here for talent, and even genius, to devise forms of beauty, in many degrees of simplicity and diversity, from the action-dialogue, or miniature drama of fifteen or thirty minutes, for younger pupils, to celebrations that might crowd a full hour or more with poetry and melody, and with phrases that will nobly haunt the soul for years afterwards.

I append one Talk which will pick up threads of the Early Age, traverse the Catholic-feudal period, and carry

---

[1] Many objects are pictured in Quennell's " History of Every-day Things in England " (1919), and J. H. Robinson's " Mediæval and Modern Times " (American ; 1916).

[2] A capital modern imitation of such maps is appended to Jeudwine's " Foundations of Society and the Land."

us into the vivid events of the nineteenth century. This illustration should serve as a further reminder that I by no means propose that the thoughts of teacher and pupils should be exclusively devoted to the Early Age, or the Catholic-feudal Age, or the Age of Expansion, as the case may be.

LESSON ON ITALY

Tan-faced country lads sit under beech trees out of the hot sun, and as, from this shady covert, they watch the meadows where sheep browse, or the hilly slopes where goats bite shrubs, they play tunes on the oaten pipe (four-hole whistle) or perhaps the seven-reed mouth-organ (Pan's pipes).[1] Cattle wander over the grass. But times are not always so quiet, for wild boars may rush from the woods, or wolves fall upon the flock. At sunset, the herdsmen pipe the home-call to their goats : " Go home, the evening star arises, my full-fed goats, go home ! " In this land of pasture and crops by the River Po, in Italy, a young man, with earnest eyes, notices the things about him—ploughmen, oxen, corn-fields, horses, cherry-trees, olives, apples, walnut, chestnut, vine and bee-hives. With reed-pen he scratches lines on waxed-wood tablets. This is the poet Virgil. Nor does he only tell of whistling shepherds and plough-oxen. He tells of terrible signs— the black smoke from Mount Etna, the howl of dogs at night, the shaking of Alps, the overflow of rivers sweeping trees and dead animals along ; and these signs happened (so the village folk said) when the great soldier and leader, Julius Cæsar was stabbed to death in Rome. Here, at

---

[1] " Tityre, tu, patulae recubans sub tegmine fagi,
Silvestrem tenui musam meditaris avena."
(Opening lines of Virgil's " Bucolics.")

Naples, by the blue sea, was this famous poet's tomb (29 B.C.).

The times go by, and we come to the days when the Crusaders wore the Red Cross, and organs played in churches; and we stand among a crowd of country folk who, on a hill-side, listen to a grey-robed preacher, and he speaks of the love of the pitying Father and Lord who sent His Son Jesus to die on the wood of the Cross. This preacher was Francis, of the City of Assisi. One day he met many birds, and spoke to them, and many more came from trees, and they made a great company on the ground, and he called them his " little sisters," and told them God gave them their food and drink. They kept silence during the sermon, and after his " Amen " they moved not. He saw they waited for a blessing, so he made the sign of the cross, and they flew away twittering.

Folk did not dare to stir out of the city of Agobio for fear of a grisly wolf that lay in wait to tear and devour. Brother Francis went out and much people followed him. With open mouth the wolf sprang at him, but stopped when Francis made the sign of the cross. " Come hither, brother wolf," he said, for to wolves, or to wolfish men, he was ever kind in look and word. Then he gently persuaded the beast to give up his cruel ways, and act as a neighbour and good citizen should; and if he promised so to act, the folk of Agobio would provide him meat and drink and lodging. Brother Wolf moved his body, tail, and eyes in token of his promise, and he, and Francis, and all the folk went into the city in peace and joy. Two years did citizen Wolf dwell there, and in friendship with all, and when he died the townsfolk sadly grieved. Perhaps, indeed, it was a brigand of the forest—wolf-like in his savage habits—whom St. Francis of Assisi touched to the heart. Now this saint of the grey robe died in 1226; and many an old church, or street, still reminds us to-day of the Grey Friars.

An Italian boy, son of a ship's captain, was born at the City of Nice, on the sea coast, in 1807. Tender-hearted was he, like to Francis. He let birds out of cages. A wounded grasshopper made him cry. He rebuked companions who crushed flowers, saying " The great spirit of eternal life is in everything." Yet I must tell you the real, horrid truth !—he played truant from school, and took a gun to shoot game on the hills. From time to time this brave youth saved sixteen lives ; the first being that of a poor washerwoman who fell into a deep ditch. As cabin-boy he sailed with his father, and himself became a ship's captain ; and, three times, he was captured by pirates, and released. His eyes were blue, his hair thick and flowing, his face lion-like ; and his name was Joseph (Giuseppe) Garibaldi.

He fled away from Italy, though he dearly loved the land of Virgil and St. Francis ; for he and other young men (one was named Mazzini), had become rebels against the armies of the white-coats, the Austrians—those Austrians who gave sore trouble to Italy till the end of the Great War in 1918. Italy was divided into several lands, and Italian hearts longed to unite them all in one. Garibaldi lived in South America for twelve years, and there, also, he was a friend of rebels, helping the people who struggled against the rule of tyrants. Once, for some hours, enemies hung him by his wrists, and great was his pain. Great also were his joys. From a ship's deck in a harbour he saw a handsome girl on the balcony of a house, and a friend introduced him to the household ; and this girl, Anita, became the wife of the lion-faced Italian.

He heard a call from Italy. Stirring were the times. He must go, he and a band of his soldiers, all clad in red shirts or jackets. They landed at Genoa, and others joined ; they marched, and more joined. A Catholic priest, the brave Ugo Bassi, preached in a city market-place, inviting youths to join Garibaldi's army of liberty, and rich men to give money. And one poor girl, having no gold to offer, cut the splendid locks of her hair that it might be sold, and the money bestowed upon the cause of Italian Unity. On the Red Shirts marched to Rome, and Garibaldi and Mazzini and their comrades declared a Republic, and the Pope had fled from the city. French and Austrians and Spaniards and Naples men circled the city, and laid siege, and broke in, and Garibaldi and his loyal followers retreated over the wooded Apennines. Anita also went in this flight of sorrow. Guns were abandoned, prisoners taken, the band became less, and few reached the Eastern waters (Adriatic Sea). Some escaped in ships, the Austrians pursuing. Garibaldi carried poor sick Anita on shore to a lonely farmhouse, where she died, and he, cut to the inmost heart with grief, went westwards, over hills and through forests, to the western coast again ; and so escaped to New York in the United States.

In New York City he worked in the stench of a candle factory. He plied a merchant vessel from port to port, and industriously saved money, and at length came eastwards again, and bought a small island, Caprera, near the larger island of Sardinia. Here he farmed a rather barren soil, where goats leaped on rocks, and cattle and sheep ate the scant grass. Sometimes as a tender shepherd, Giuseppe would go forth into the night to seek a stray lamb and bear it home on his shoulders rejoicing.

Again sounded the alarm of war ! Again men sought to make Italy one. From Genoa, a thousand Red Shirts sailed to the orange-growing and vine-growing island of Sicily (1860). Englishmen joined this army also. Through Sicily fared the Red Shirts—the people cheering—and over the water to the mainland, and so to Naples city, where Garibaldi greeted the King, Victor Emmanuel—once King of Sardinia—and now King of almost all Italy. Even the horses of Naples were glad—for when Garibaldi observed their thin and half-starved condition, he gave a soldier's orders that all owners and drivers should treat their horses with mercy and good food.

To London ! For six hours, Garibaldi sat in a carriage, that moved very slowly along the crowded streets, and people shook hands with the Italian hero ; thousands shook hands ; and coloured pictures of the Red-Shirt General and his white horse were hung on many an English wall.

In 1870, the French guards quitted Rome, and Victor Emmanuel and his troops entered, and Rome has since been the capital of United Italy. Mazzini rejoiced, as Italy's friend. The French had gone to meet the rush of the German invaders. Garibaldi, who once had fought the French, now rallied to their aid, and, with a regiment of Red Shirts, took a part in defending the French Republic ; for Garibaldi loved republics.

After that, as farmer once again in Caprera, he lived a peaceful life, and his health slowly failed.   From his window he gazed on granite rocks and the rippling sea.   As he lay dying (1882), two little birds that were wont to peck crumbs from his hand, twittered noisily on the sill of the bedroom window, and his friends were about to drive the birds away.

" Let them in," said Garibaldi ; " and remember to feed them when I am gone."

CHAPTER IV

THE AGE OF EXPANSION

(1300 TO THE WORLD-WAR, 1914–1918, AND THE LEAGUE
OF NATIONS, 1919).

TO the stage of childhood which is passing into adolescence, the story of the Age of Expansion should bear a peculiar inspiration ; for growth appeals to the growing soul. This period of six hundred years has been " revolutionary." I often doubt, however, the basic value of the term " revolutionary." To an Egyptian or Minoan, the Greek-Roman Age would have seemed one of extraordinary change. And Pericles or Cæsar, viewing Europe in the days of Parliaments, Universities, and Dante, would have felt no little amazement at unexpected perturbations and upheavals. And I incline to the judgment that posterity, so far from setting much store by our European and American " revolutions," our Renascences, and our wars, will rather find the chief interest in the steady opening of all corners of the globe to civilization until the Poles were touched by human feet, and every wilderness was disclosed to the invincible human eye. It is possible that, if the Muse of History had told us an ampler tale, we should hear of as many " revolutions " in the Ages of Stone and Bronze as in the Age of Luther, Cromwell, Washington, Mirabeau, and Lenin. This is

83

not to say that the word " revolution " should be erased from the records ; but the word stands for a quite secondary factor in the impressive story. The chief lesson is one of a constantly unfolding order, whose name is civilization.   Auguste Comte, after a long survey of history, said that a synthetic view gives one a consoling sense of a law of increasing regularity in the human order, or evolution.

While such may be our philosophic thoughts, we do not express ourselves in such phrases to young learners. But we can so frame the story of mankind, in its older, and newer, and newest testaments, as to create an unformulated sentiment of faith in the steady march of man's soul through pain, purgatorial fire, and ever clearer visions.   How is it possible to form such a conviction by haphazard dips into one sort of " history " to-day, and another sort to-morrow ?   I have, in a previous page, stated my view that, in logical and consistent method, the Catholic instruction based on the Bible was, relatively to its period, entirely sound.   It began with the Beginning of things and the Unveiling of Light, and it pursued its undaunted course to the dream of a finally reorganized and purified society.

The earlier records of humanity are, naturally, full of legends, which furnish rich material for the exercise of young people's moral and intellectual judgment.   In the Age of Expansion we approach a much larger revelation of exact science.   It is meet that minds on the threshold of adolescence, and more and more disposed (if education allows scope and freedom), to apply reason to nature and experience, should be encouraged to study the Age which produced Copernicus, Galileo, Newton, Lavoisier, Faraday, Darwin, Fabre, Le Play,

Pasteur, Lister. But the love of poetry, which was born with the love of legends, will remain to beautify this new movement of reason. Our science, our geography, our economics, will mainly emerge through biography; that is, through the spell or gospel of human courage, wisdom, determination, faith. The lessons absorbed in the years 12 to 14, or so, will inspire the soul towards the systematic training in science, and the systematic training in æsthetic, in citizenship and in social service, which all nations should provide for all their sons and daughters . . . though I feel, acutely enough, that here I speak as a visionary.

I repeat the order of educational values implied all through my proposals—first, moral training, then æsthetic, then intellectual, then practical (that is, directed towards daily industry and social service). At the beginning of each stage, 1 have placed economic themes, relating to plants, animals, minerals, agriculture, manufacture, and the status of the labourer. If I wanted to quote precedents, I might cite Comte's selection of the Nutritive Instinct as the basis of psychology, or Marx's doctrine of the Materialist Basis of History, or, in the Biblical epic, the gardening and tillage of the Adamic world, and the carpentry and shepherding of the Christian, coupled with a very concrete note on Daily Bread in the Lord's Prayer. At the outset of this book, I described normal education as aiming at service " expressed through industry." I meant that the whole economic field and life should be consecrated by this ideal. Morality, art, science, philosophy, and religion constitute civilization, but they must play their part on the material stage, and can never play their best part until each citizen roots his citizenhood in his personal service in one form or another of many-sided industry.

The Age of Expansion discovers or emphasizes tea, coffee, beet, rubber, esparto, the soya bean of eastern Asia, and the American products, potato, maize, cocoa, arrowroot, quinine, tomato, pineapple, maté (Paraguay tea), alpaca, etc. ; palm oil and mineral oils ; mulberry and silk culture ; nitrate, soda, sulphuric acid, extended gold-mining, aluminium, radium, etc.   All such products have their historical and human, and oft-times pathetic and romantic associations.   Take soda as an example :

Nicholas Leblanc, b. 1742, near Bourges, studied surgery, chemistry ; experimented in making soda from common salt. In 1794, the Committee of Public Safety abolished his patent rights.   Leblanc served the Republic as special officer, improving cotton-machinery, ship-building, hospitals, mining, alum-manufacture, police-system, education.   Of 3,000 francs promised him as public compensation, he received only 600. Soda factory restored to him, 1801, but others competed. Heart-broken, he shot himself, 1806.   His widow died, 1829, having vainly tried to obtain from Government the money due to her husband.   Paris street named after Leblanc in 1856 ; bronze statue, 1887.   (" Life," by his grandson Anastasi, 1884). An immense area of research for what may be called " Economic Stories," is open to enterprising teachers.   Economic history has its tragedy, comedy, lyrics, and apocalypses.

Even in a talk with younger children we have had a glimpse of a great Roman poet who found in agriculture (" Georgics," Earth-labour ; the work, so to say, of George the husbandman), a theme for poetry.   Agriculture is one of the finest world-dramas, yet it has been sadly despised by the stage-managers of our educational theatre.   I wonder how many English village children, who have suffered under lists of Plantagenet kings, or been bored with all-too-elaborate " sums " in corn-measure, have ever heard of the work, or even the names, of such apostolic farmers as Jethro Tull, Robert Bakewell, and Arthur Young ?[1]   It is quite possible to render anecdotal outlines of the careers of such Georgic Masters interesting to girls and boys ; and pictures by Potter, Cuyp, George Morland, and other painters of rural scenes, would lend pleasant commentaries. And is there no glory in the tale of forestry, of the work of Kew Gardens, or of the irrigation of wastes in Australia, India, Mesopotamia, Egypt, United States ? Or in the marvellous horticulture of Luther Burbank, in his enchanted gardens of California ? Clio, the Muse of History, has duly recorded the lives of Lawes and Gilbert, and of Joseph Arch ; but one may safely assume that, to vast crowds of British citizens (and to not a few teachers ?), these three names convey no message.

Sir John Bennet Lawes (1814–1900) and Dr. Joseph H. Gilbert (1817–1901), worked together for fifty-seven years, at the Rothamsted Experimental Farm, near St. Albans, in research into the chemistry of soils and plants, scientific manuring, etc., and Lawes left £100,000 to carry on the enterprise. Government now assists. In October, 1919, new laboratories were opened, and the station is now one of the most important centres in the world. For biographical details of much interest, see Sir A. D. Hall's " Book of the Rothamsted Experiments " (1917).

Joseph Arch (1826–1919), born at Barford, near Stratford-on-Avon, son of industrious shepherd, who earned 8s. to 10s. a week. Mother taught him Shakespeare and Bible. As a child, scandalized to see smocked labourers taking Communion in church separately from squire, farmers, etc. Champion hedge-cutter of England. Wesleyan local preacher. In 1872, formed Labourers' Union, which grew into National Agricultural Labourers' Union. Procession, strikes for 16s., etc. Condemned Game Laws, encouraged emigration, advocated education. M.P. for N.W. Norfolk, 1885 and 1892. Died, aged 92, in cottage he was born in. (Autobiography, edited by Lady Warwick, 1898 ; full of lively episodes).

[1] Salient particulars are given in Traill's " Social History of England. " vol. 5.

I regret giving these biographies in so severely abridged versions.[1]

Geographical expansion may be indicated in these running notes : Caravan routes in Asia ; Venetian commerce in Oriental wares; slaves ; piracy gradually suppressed ; compass in general use in the fourteenth, century ; Madeira discovered, 1419 ; Azores settled 1448 ; story of Sindbad (date about 1500 perhaps) ; Bartholomew Diaz sails round the Cape, 1486 ; Vasco da Gama's voyage to India, 1498 ; [2] Columbus ; Conquest of Mexico and Peru ; Hakluyt's " Voyages " ; More's " Utopia "; Magellan's circumnavigation, 1519–21 ; Mercator's map ; Drake ; Tamburlaine's dying thought of a canal between the Red and Terrene (Mediterranean) Seas :

> " I meant to cut a channel to them both,
> That men might quickly sail to India."

(quoted by Prof. W. Raleigh in his " English Voyagers," from Marlowe's play) ; East India Company ; Defoe's " Robinson Crusoe " as a sign of interest in distant regions ; Captain Cook ; Mungo Park ; Livingstone ; Stanley ; Nansen ; Peary ; Amundsen ; Scott ; explorations of Sturt and others in Australia. Foundation of United States ; pathfinders of the American " West " ; Bates's Wanderings on the Amazons ; Darwin's Voyage. Canals : French, English, Suez, Panama. Railroads,

---

[1] About 1918, I applied to various well-known Irish scholars for references to works containing biographies of Irish notables, especially agriculturists, or workers at a craft, e.g., linen. I received lists of saints, patriots, M.P.'s, novelists, and poets, but not one name of a farmer, craftsman, etc. There is, however, a growing literature on Irish Agricultural Organization.

[2] Fully described on the basis of Camoens' " Lusiads " in my " Conduct Stories " (Allen & Unwin).

English, American, Siberian. Roads constructed by Metcalf and others. Sailing ships, steam, oil. Sea-routes ; lighthouses ; air-routes. Alpine and other mountain-climbing. Vast extension of oversea migration ; colonies in America, Africa, Australia, New Zealand ; labours of Hindu coolies, Lascars, Japanese, Chinese, negroes, outside their native lands. Serious " colour " and labour questions that arise.[1]

The Age gave us companies, banks, interest (as distinct from " usury "), wages-system, profit-making on capital. Rudimentary ideas about taxes, budgets, rates, and tariffs, can be imparted. Decimal coinage. Metric system, first mooted by James Watt, Franklin, Jefferson, and French scientists. " Notes," originating in goldsmiths' receipts for gold deposited in their keeping and used in negotiation. First bank-note issued by Swedish bank, 1658. Compare use of gold in craft (as by Benvenuto Cellini) and in coinage. Instructive case of Spain, which captured enormous quantities of precious metals in America, but (her own products and manufactures being few) exchanged gold and silver for Dutch and English goods, and was in the end no richer through her New World " wealth."[2] The realm of money is not without its touches of biographical interest, as in the case of Jacques Cœur :

Jacques Cœur, born at Bourges, 1395, visited Syria as trader, the French exchanging tin, lead, copper, cloth, for oak-galls, silk, indigo, sugar, soap, goatskins, carpets. In Royal Mints at Bourges and Paris, coined gold and silver coins. Tax-collector salt-inspector, paper-maker ; money-lender to King and others.

[1] For general views of Human Geography, see works by Sir H. H. Johnston, C. R. Enock, Geddes, and Branford, and, in French, Brunhes.

[2] See W. A. Shaw's " History of the Currency." Children, aged 12 to 14, can understand this important example.

Had coat-of-arms showing a heart (*cœur*). Built palace with hearts on walls and windows. Rode in processions, dressed in scarlet velvet, with ruby on sword-hilt. Accused by enemies ; degraded ; knelt bare-headed, holding candle of penance, before royal officer. Joins war against Turks, dies in Chios Isle, 1356. Note that he was contemporary with Joan of Arc.

An English type of mercantile genius would be Gresham (1519-1579).

This Age marks the decline of serfdom and the Peasants' Rising of 1381. The change was a healthy one. The life of England was growing more vigorous. And at this very time, modern English poetry was born with Chaucer, whose " Canterbury Tales," in selection, should be narrated when dealing with the social events of that century (14th). So again, when England is seen expanding in trade, in its self-confidence under Spanish threats and peril, and in its exploring temper, suitable stories from Shakespeare should be introduced as part of the general movement, rather than be set aside for formal treatment in a " literature " lesson.

The eighteenth century brings the extension of machinery, and Industrial Revolution, 1750 or so, to (let us say as a turning-point) 1914. While honesty requires that some of the social evils, such as overwork, child labour, unemployment, and pauperism, should be described, it would seem advisable to direct young people's thoughts to the historical and biographical factors, e.g., story of Trade Unions and Trade Union pioneers, such as Francis Place ; the story of the Co-operative Movement from the days of Owen and the Rochdale Pioneers onwards ; and the story of certain typical chartists, such as Lovett, and Socialists, such as Marx, Morris, Hyndman. The lives of leading inventors should be told—Montgolfier, Vaucanson, Watt, Stephenson, Jacquard, Edison, Marconi ; and they should be told as illustrations of genius and service, apart from the commercial aspects. Comte proposed an annual Festival of Machines ; and Dr. Hayward presents an example, dedicated to .the Art of Flying (aeroplanes, etc.), in his " School Celebrations." Let a simple comparison be drawn between the Labour difficulties in England in Elizabethan times (suppression of " vagabonds," Poor Law introduced) and the inclusion of a Labour Department in the League of Nations, 1919, and the first meeting of this " International " at Washington. And here again, such " literature " as the children can appreciate should accompany the social march of the period in which the authors created. Gray's noble " Elegy," Burns's lyrics, Dickens's tales, and Tennyson's poems expressed the deepening sense of humanity ; just as Scott expressed the quickened interest in the romance of history. It was no accident that Scott was contemporary with Gibbon, though this comment, of course, is not proposed for the notice of children.

The industrial theme connects with public and domestic sanitation and hygiene ; hospitals, nursing, care of lunatics and feeble-minded, municipal cleanliness, war against food adulteration, better housing, townplanning, war against malaria, yellow fever, plague, sleeping-sickness. This noble effort of life against death is symbolized by such names as John Howard, Pinel, Simpson, Chadwick, Pasteur, Lister, Manson, Ross, Reed, Gorgas, Ebenezer Howard, Florence Nightingale, Elsie Inglis. And it is a subject of congratulation that sex-hygiene, approached on the positive side by the spirit of chivalry and self-discipline, and, on the negative, by such organizations as the

Council for Combating Venereal Disease, should occupy so much serious public attention in the present day.

Sir Ronald Ross, born 1857, when an army surgeon at Bangalore, studied the causes of the malaria fever which slew a million people annually in India. He traced the disease to a parasite in the body of a species of mosquito, whose bite both injects the parasite into human blood, and carries it from one fever-patient to another. The remedy lies in exterminating the mosquito, and this work is now extensively pursued in tropical regions. During his minute research, Ross wrote :

> " I know this little thing
> A myriad men will save.
> O Death, where is thy sting ?
> Thy victory, O grave ? "

Sir Ronald has been called " the apostle of tropical sanitation." The reduction of yellow fever by suppressing the mosquito made Panama healthier, and rendered the construction of the canal finally possible. (See Gregory's " Discovery," and descriptions of the labours of Reed and Gorgas).

The broad field of religion may be indicated : The double stream of Puritan movement (with Church of England or Anglo-Catholic aspects) and Roman Catholic movement ; on the one side, life-stories of Wiclif, Latimer, Milton, Bunyan, Wesley, Quakers, Huguenots, Pilgrim Fathers, and Missions ; on the other side, St. Teresa, St. C. Borromeo, Loyola and the Jesuit Martyrs, St. Vincent de Paul, and many Roman Missions. The enumeration of these parallel series will shock narrow sectaries, and will be serenely welcomed by all who understand the inspiration of Humanity's Story. The help of pictures (Raphael, Rubens, Rembrandt, Poussin, Millet of the " Angelus," Blake, Doré, Burne-Jones, Millais, and others) should be constantly invoked. In the literary field, we note the history of the English Bible, the works of Milton and Bunyan, and some of

Byron's poems. Where possible, hints may be drawn from church music, historic hymns, and Handel's Oratorios. Modern folk-lore selections, Slav and others, often present naïve and homely religious themes. An outline story of the Jews should be sympathetically given, and also (for Great Britain especially) an account of various " emancipations " of Catholics, Quakers, Nonconformists generally, and of Charles Bradlaugh and the House of Commons, etc. And the teachers should devote systematic thought to establishing cordial feeling between " East and West," the most important means being the recital of the good lives and teachings of ancient and modern Hindus, Buddhists, Mohammedans, and Confucians.[1]

Simple details of education would be such as these : Pictures of Grammar Schools, of which England had about 300 before the Reformation, and a passage from Stow (1633), describing a public exercise of Grammar School boys who assembled at a bench under a church-yard tree, one scholar standing up to display his knowledge until vanquished by a cleverer companion, and so on.[2] If a few examples from the picture-book of Comenius (1592-1671), and a sketch of that excellent teacher's life could be presented, it would be a proper tribute to his merits. A brief account of Charity Schools (not forgetting Blake's verses, " 'Twas on a Holy Thursday, their innocent faces clean," and his later lines, " Is this a holy thing to see ? ") would lead up to the story of Board, Council, and other schools. Add notices of the work of Pestalozzi and Froebel. And why

[1] " The British Empire contains more Mohammedans than Christians, and nearly three times as many Hindus." Sir Francis Younghusband, in " England's Mission " (1919).

[2] Foster Watson's " Old Grammar Schools " (1916).

not a history of games, toys, and toymakers, and of Hans Andersen, Louisa Alcott, and other writers for the young ? The labour of the noble Abbé de l'Epée, teacher of the deaf and dumb, deserves one or two passing anecdotes. And " the greatest of machines " (as Dr. J. H. Bridges names the printing-press) should have a place in the tale of learning, together with a flying view of the progress of newspapers, books, magazines, and illustrations.

I will rapidly enumerate names that call up the salient phases of art, craft, and literature in this Age : Miracle-plays, Froissart, Arras tapestries, Donatello, St. George's Chapel at Windsor, Hampton Court, St. Peter's at Rome, Albrecht Dürer, Angelo, Raphael, Titian, civic buildings of Flanders, Palissy, Cervantes, Calderon, Shakespeare, Murillo, Rubens, Rembrandt, Wren, Defoe, Grinling Gibbons, Bartolozzi, Hogarth, Reynolds, Gainsborough, Blake, Morland, Bewick, Sèvres earthenware, Wedgwood, lace-making, fine furniture and clocks,—

Thomas Tompion, clockmaker, of London, gave a clock, in 1709, to the Pump Room at Bath ; still going at end of nineteenth century. A person once brought a watch to him to be repaired. It bore Tompion's name. Tompion examined it, detected fraudulent use of his name, smashed watch with hammer, and gave astonished customer a new and genuine one. Such was the craftsman's splendid pride.

Turner, Madox Brown, Crane, Dickens, Kingsley, Longfellow, Tennyson, Kipling—and many others such. With regard to the craftsmen and artists here named, the educator should, at this stage, rely upon printed pictures, and (for some purposes still better) magic lantern slides, coloured if possible. But I am bound to emphasize once more my judgment that the great masterpieces of literature, painting, etc., are most naturally and instructively studied in immediate association with the social events and atmospheres in which they were produced, and not in artificial series of " Literature lessons," " Art lessons," etc.[1] Every town of considerable size (access by villagers not being overlooked) should possess a popular theatre like the famous " Old Vic " (Old Victoria Theatre) in South London, where school children, as well as adults, can witness, free or cheaply, Shakesperean and other classical plays, pageants, morality plays, Nativity plays, and the like. I should add selected scenes from the York, Wakefield, Chester, or Coventry cycles of the fourteenth to sixteenth centuries, including Creation, Flood, Gospel episodes, Apocryphal Gospel stories, and mediæval legends.[2] And one could wish for occasional displays of some of the beautiful " autos " of the Spanish poet Calderon (1600–1681), a contemporary of Shakespeare, Milton, and Bunyan. For example, Calderon represents Adam, who has just been expelled from Paradise, as beseeching the help of the four Seasons. None of them offers him a free gift. But yet they help. Spring gives him a spade to dig, and the angel Gabriel appears, holding the lily of the Annunciation. Summer hands him a sickle in readiness for harvest, and John the Baptist comes forth as forerunner of the Divine Sun. Autumn points to vines that need culture, and also registers the birthday of Mary. Winter comes as an aged shepherd with a crook, as a reminder of the herds-

[1] C. R. Ashbee has published three admirable charts of " Arts and Crafts " of Renascence, 16th, 17th, and 18th centuries. In the realm of æsthetic, Mr. Ashbee has done for students what the Grand Old Man of Ancoats (Manchester), Charles Rowley, has done for popular recreation.

[2] Amply described in A. W. Pollard's " English Miracle Plays." 4th edition, (1904.)

man's labour, and promises the splendour of angels singing the Nativity and world-peace. In other words, humanity must link its ideals with its self-reliance and industry. Even if we do not reproduce Calderon's " autos," we may draw hints from his rich sources.[1]

For music, children aged 12 to 14, or so, cannot do better than learn the English, Welsh, Scottish, Irish, and other songs, consecrated by the sure test of popular taste.[2]

In science, besides the sanitary pioneers already marked, we have—Copernicus, Galileo, Harvey, Newton, Réaumur, Franklin, Priestley, Linnæus, Lavoisier, Darwin, Wallace, Hooker, Faraday, Joule, Hertz, Röntgen, and so on ; all being introduced by way of biographical anecdote and sketch, with portraits whenever possible ; and always, as far as can be, in relation to their period.[3] Some teachers would be interested in reciting an outline of the work of Zamenhof (1859–1917), the inventor of Esperanto. And at this point, a few illustrated talks on geology, and the researches of W. Smith, C. Lyell, etc., would lead to an explanation of our " Table of Time Before Man." The Geological Society (British) was founded in 1807, and public interest in Early man practically arose in the two or three generations that followed.

Of political events, with which children's " history lessons " have hitherto been too painfully laden, only a few outstanding types need be considered : The three great English defences : against Spain, France

[1] See E. J. Hasell's " Calderon " (1879).
[2] With the help of such societies as the " League of the Arts," there is now no difficulty in the choice.
[3] For types of material, see Sir R. A. Gregory's " Discovery, the Spirit and Service of Science."

(Louis XIV and Napoleon), and Germany (1914-1918); English (Cromwellian) revolution, growth of British Commonwealth,[1] American and French Revolutions, extension of British suffrage, rise of S. American Republics, Italian Unity, Rise of Japan, American Civil War (1861–1865), and abolition everywhere of negro-slavery. In the case of the American Civil War, the story of the life of Abraham Lincoln would cover all the facts comprehensible at this stage. These events are duly recorded in our preliminary " Table." They readily carry us forward to the conception of vast international co-operations in exhibitions, congresses, Postal Union, Red Cross Work, and the League of Nations.

Associated with this long course of historical instruction (the sole " subject " taught) will be activities, the bare mention of which will now suffice : Reading at home, in school, and in connexion with Juvenile Libraries ; writing of original letters, recollections, tales, perhaps poems ; drawing, painting, modelling, experiments in physics and chemistry, with a view to fostering a scientific spirit, not to studying formal " science " ; mapping, excursions, " regional survey " :

A Board of Education (Welsh Department) scheme (1919), for " the collection of rural lore in Wales," invited teachers and children to co-operate in collecting traditions and facts as to local industries, agriculture, pastoral life, religion, education, local worthies, wild life, antiquities, customs, proverbs, legends, dialects, folk-lore, etc., with the ordnance map as a basis. Plenty of suggestions can be obtained from the Outlook Tower, Edinburgh, or the Regional Association, London. Prof. Patrick Geddes is a moving spirit in both institutions.

And arithmetic (taking due note of the decimal

[1] " Which we used to call Empire." Prince of Wales in 1920.

point, first used by Napier, who died 1617) will cover household needs, elementary business transactions, coupled with simple but adequate notions of balance sheets, budgets, rates, taxes, profit-system, labour and value, price, capital. All this calculating and economic apparatus must be esteemed as a machine for efficiency and honesty in the service of the Public Good, and for integrity of private earning, saving, or outlay. Grossly immoral and irreligious is the fashion of treating mathematical faculties and exercises as a field detached from the great issues of duty and fellowship. The astronomy which frames a Nautical Almanac and ascertains the position of ships, both for guidance and salvation of voyagers, should be a symbol of the submission of the whole art of logic, including arithmetic, to the welfare of society.[1]   And in days to come, this submission will be one of the striking themes of the School Celebrations which (as Dr. Hayward has so earnestly urged) should beautify and consecrate the thought and life of teachers and learners. In using the term " teachers," I think of parents also, and particularly of the mothers. The moralization of the educational process will never be fulfilled except with the powerful help of women's sympathy, definitely concentrated and expressed in home co-operation, and in public declaration.

Treat the scheme, from the Infants' School stage to the threshold of adolescence, with elasticity. Choose those elements that suit your gifts in teaching, and the special capacities of your pupils. Never lose hold of

---

[1] An Italian writer, Baldi, invents the Fable : "A pair of compasses, being asked why, in order to draw a circle, one foot stood and the other moved, replied, ' Constancy and work must go together.' "   It is a little fanciful, but conveys a hint as to methods.

the prime purpose of personal and social service. At each step enlist the aid of beauty, and seek to train the spirit of rationality—never forgetting that rationality is expressed through the imagination (a quite different thing from wandering fancy) as well as through science. The master-thought being responsibility towards " family, country, and humanity," this second term, " country," necessarily gives rise to local variations. The French teacher, the American, the Indian, the Australian, and the rest, will modify details. Nevertheless, the broad chronology of the Ages, and the general framework, should stand for all schools of civilization alike. The Table with which we set out should be continually referred to, and events and persons allocated to the Early Age, or the Feudal, or the Modern. Such allocation will, in the case of younger children, be extremely tentative and faint, moderately practicable at the age of ten or so, and, under common-sense limitations, systematic at the age 12 to 14, and later.

In the case of lessons previously placed before the reader (India, Ireland, Rhone, Italy), I took unusual leaps along the Ages, in order to symbolize the value of a connected historical view, to be set before the educator as an ideal to be approximately realized. The three biographical themes here following are normal lessons (divisible, of course, into two or more talks each). The growing map will accompany each lesson ; literature and life go together ; each topic, in one way or another, points to duty and service ; each is, fundamentally, a history lesson.

LESSON ON MILTON

You know how Guido Fawkes tried to blow up the Parliament House by the river at Westminster, in 1605. If you walked from Westminster, past St. Martin's green fields along the shore, or Strand, of the Thames, you would come to the street of shops, Cheapside. A turning off was Bread Street, where in 1608, in a house before which the sign of the " Spread Eagle " hung, a baby was born to Mr. and Mrs. Milton. Baby John grew into a studious boy, who tried his eyes by candle light, reading books till one o'clock in the morning. Very ready was he to learn from his father to play the organ and talk Latin. Often he sat alone, making verses. He could " build the lofty rhyme," like this :

> Let us, with a gladsome mind,
> Praise the Lord, for He is kind ;
> For His mercies aye endure,
> Ever faithful, ever sure.

Then he went to the city where the colleges of Cambridge University stand by the river *Camus*, which runs among sedges, and through the grassy pastures. His great friend was Edward King, with whom he read books, and talked of England's people, and how the people were like to sheep that needed good shepherds, that is, good teachers, priests, poets ; and Edward hoped to be such a shepherd. The good shepherd would spend no time in idle feasts, but would work hard to train himself as a wise teacher. He would "scorn delights and live laborious days." He would play his oaten flute, or Pan's pipe, and all the while watch that the flock had good pasture. But careless shepherds would think of their own pleasures and purse more than the people's weal, and the "hungry sheep look up and are not fed."

One day, in 1637, as John Milton was passing a quiet

time in a village near Windsor, shocking news came. Edward King had been drowned in a ship that was crossing the Irish Sea near Chester. His body was never found; but Milton gathered leaves of "laurel, myrtle brown, and ivy," as if to strew over his dead friend's grave.

Across the plains of France, John travelled, and over the Alps into sunny Italy. There he visited the aged astronomer, Galileo, through whose telescope he peeped at the spotty globe of the moon. But, as he journeyed in fair scenes and fine cities, tidings arrived of trouble and storm in England, of the quarrels of Parliament and King, of men preparing to fight against a bad rule. He hurried home, for, said he, " I thought it base, whilst my countrymen were fighting for liberty, that I should be travelling abroad to improve my mind."[1]

At the Council of State, where Cromwell sat as chief, guiding the affairs of the Commonwealth of England, Milton, sat, pen in hand, writing as Secretary. One of his " Lofty Rhymes " began, "Cromwell, our chief of men." At other times Milton could be seen at a house with a pleasant garden in front, where boys listened as pupils to his lessons. Then sad times befell, and his eyes darkened into blindness; and one of his daughters was deformed, and a great plague overshadowed London, and many folks died. Milton's sorrows were greater through the death of Cromwell, and the coming back of Charles II as King—for no good king and shepherd was he.

In a country cottage, at Chalfont St. Giles, in Buckinghamshire—still kept carefully, with its windows of small panes, its gables, and flower-garden—blind Milton would think and repeat verses to himself, and then dictate the verses for others to write. Thus he made his great poem of " Paradise Lost," which told how Adam and Eve ate the Forbidden Fruit, and were driven from the happy garden:

> " They, hand in hand, with wandering steps and slow
> Through Eden took their solitary way."

[1] Wars or no wars, this most noble sentence has a message for all educators.

Towards the close of the poet's life, he dwelt in London. When the weather was mild, he would sit at the door, clad in a coarse, grey coat, receiving callers. Indoors, his dress was black. Every afternoon music was played to him. At evening, he smoked a pipe, drank a glass of water, and retired to bed. To his eyes, night and morn were alike. He died in 1674, and was buried in Bunhill Fields, where John Bunyan was also buried later. And, if you ever pass the church of St. Giles, Cripplegate, you will see a statue of Milton, with eyes that are blind, and yet look afar, and see "things invisible to mortal sight."

You remember the friend who was drowned. One morning, in fancy, Milton went into the quiet green country, sad with the memory of his dead companion. Clad in a blue mantle, he passed among trees, picking leaves of "laurel, myrtle, and ivy," with which to strew a coffin or a grave. The poet would play on his flute, and make rhyming lines in a solemn song to "Lycidas," his friend. That friend, whom he knew so well at Cambridge, had been a poet-singer too :

> " Who would not sing for Lycidas ? He knew,
> Himself, to sing, and build the lofty rhyme."

Milton and Lycidas had once played happy music on oaten flutes together, in sunlight and by starlight. But Lycidas has gone away :

> " But oh ! the heavy change, now thou art gone,
> Now thou art gone, and never must return."

" Ah ! " says Milton, " when my friend was drowning, why did not the ocean-queens—the nymphs of the sea— hear his cry, and rush to his help ? Where were ye, Nymphs ? "

At Cambridge, Lycidas had studied his books, and, like Milton, laboured so hard to learn the business of shepherd- ing the sheep, of teaching the people. They scorned delights, and lived laborious days. Then came this dread- ful shipwreck. The ship must have been built on a dark day, when men spoke evil words :

> " It was that fatal and perfidious bark,
> Built in the eclipse, and rigged with curses dark."

Who is this old man, clad in rough mantle, and a cap woven of sedges ? It is Camus, the spirit of the river, mourning for the young man who so often walked on the bank of the stream.

Who is this figure carrying two keys, a gold key to open doors, and an iron key to shut ? This is the apostle Peter, once boatman of the Galilean Lake. He opens a joyful gate to good shepherds, and shuts the iron gate upon the bad. Lycidas was a good teacher. Alas ! he is dead. Other men are wretched shepherds, and to them " the hungry sheep look up and are not fed." And in the war-days of Cromwell, how much were wise teachers needed for the people of England !

Come, let us gather bright flowers to strew over the grave of Lycidas—if we suppose his grave is here—primroses, jessamine, pansy, violet, musk rose, cowslips, daffodils. And as we scatter the flowers, we will tell one another that he lives again :

> " Weep no more, woeful shepherds, weep no more,
> For Lycidas, your sorrow, is not dead."

He has soared to the Heaven where bright rivers flow among groves, and songs sweetly ring in the blest kingdoms of joy and love. Nor will he forget the ships and the folk of the earth below. He will often stand on the sea-shore to protect the voyagers.

> " Now, Lycidas, the shepherds weep no more,
> Henceforth, thou art the Genius of the shore."

For, indeed, if Edward King could come to earth, he would love to guard folk from the perilous flood and the evils of the day and night.

So sings the poet. So he fingers his rhyming pipe till the sun sets, and he pulls his cloak about him against the evening chill, and he ends his poem as the day ends, and goes homewards, thinking of the other woods and fields that he must travel across to-morrow.

" And now the sun had stretched out all the hills,
And now was dropped into the western bay.
At last he rose, and twitched his mantle blue ;
To-morrow to fresh woods, and pastures new."

Such was Milton's great heart, and such his poet's lay.

Many years later, another poet, fingering another shepherd's pipe, said, " Milton ! thou shouldst be living at this hour ! England hath need of thee."

But Milton does live at this hour, if the youth of England is moved by his manly spirit.

LESSON ON GEORGE WASHINGTON

The sun glows very warm over this farmhouse, and the fields where negroes pluck weeds and remove worms so that the tobacco crops may flourish. This is Virginian tobacco. The owner of the farm is a widow, Mrs. Washington. Her boy, George (born 1732), went out early one morning with companions, and they amused themselves by capturing a stubborn colt. George put a bit in the animal's mouth, urged it to a gallop, the creature leaped wildly, fell dead. At breakfast, Mrs. Washington's reference to the colt produced silence.

" The colt is dead, madam," said George. " I killed him."

The mother flushed angrily, but said :

" I rejoice in my son who always speaks the truth."

As a young man, he measured fields and estates, drew plans, and drew them well. Just as he was a good land surveyor, so also he was a good soldier. Aged twenty-one, he was Major, and talked with solemn Indians who smoked long pipes while he urged them to join the British side against the French. With one companion he made a raft, and floated on a river on which ice-floes violently crashed.

He built a road in a wilderness. For nine hours he and his troop defended a fort against French attack, and were then allowed to march away. He followed General Braddock into the forest, where the British red-coats were encountered by Redskins and French. Braddock fell, and by torch-light Washington read the burial service over the dead leader.

Having married Mrs. Curtis, he settled to farming at Mount Vernon, where a fine house, with white-painted pillars (still preserved), looked out on the estate. Farmer Washington farmed well, and joined his white and black labourers in their industry, and cared for them in their sicknesses. The State of Virginia had a Parliament, or House of Burgesses, and of this our farmer became a member, but, at his entrance, he made but a poor speech in reply to the welcome given him as a good citizen and soldier. " Sit down, Mr. Washington," said the chairman. " Your modesty equals your valour." Fifteen years, the master of Mount Vernon served in the House of Burgesses. Great was the stir in Virginia and all along the shores of New England, for the King and Parliament in London were in an angry mood with the American Colonists, and men talked of rebellion against the British Rule, and breaking away with a new flag, and with proud independence.

In these stormy years, loyal friends took counsel with Washington as to what best to do in times that tried men's souls. Such were Jefferson, Adams, Thomas Paine, and Benjamin Franklin.

A sturdy fellow was Franklin, whose forefathers had dwelt in the villages of our Northamptonshire. Aged seventeen, he trudged into Philadelphia City, and hungry was he, as he searched for work in the printing business. For threepence, he bought three puffy big rolls, and marched along the street, one roll under the left arm, a second under the right, and eating the third ; and Miss Read, a lass who was afterwards his wife, looked from her father's door, and smiled at Benjamin's odd appearance. He was very industrious, and had great good sense, and rose to be a scientific man (inventing the lightning con-ductor), a wise statesman in war and peace, a writer of

books. It was he who first said, " Time is money," " God
helps them that help themselves," " Early to bed and
early to rise, makes a man healthy, wealthy, and wise,"
" Little strokes fell great oaks."[1]

In Philadelphia, on July 4th, 1776, Liberty Bell (still
preserved, though cracked) clanged its clang over land and
sea, and citizens crowded to the red-brick house (Independence Hall, Chestnut Street), from the steps of which
men read from a parchment roll the rolling words of the
Declaration of Independence. The British Parliament had
imposed taxes without the Colonists' consent, and so—
" We mutually pledge to each other our lives, our fortunes,
and our sacred honour." Liberty Bell—swords, muskets,
cannon—rebellion !

General George Washington, in blue uniform with buff
facings, reviewed his American troops, and the seven years'
war began (1776–1783). There had already been a fight
with redcoats at Bunker's Hill, Boston,[2] and hard strife
followed. In order to attack the enemy by surprise,
Washington's boat crossed the Delaware, when the river
was dangerous with tossing ice. At Valley Forge his men
passed a sad winter, short of food and clothing ; yet his
courage never faltered, however cold the snow or dark the
day. Lafayette, in blue and silver uniform, brought his
brave heart and cheering message from France ; and
America never forgets Lafayette. In 1783, Great Britain
acknowledged the Independence of the United States,
Washington rode to Philadelphia, gave account of his
spendings in the War, took no fee for himself, and retired
to his farm at Mount Vernon. Twice—four years each
time—he was President of the United States of America
(U.S.A.). The country had now its National Law, or
Constitution, and this law begins thus : " We, the people
of the United States, in order to form a more perfect

---

[1] Franklin's " Autobiography," and " Poor Richard's
Almanac " are real literature ; not liquid gold like Plato's, but
solid and useful pewter, and eminently characteristic of the
eighteenth century.

[2] In 1911, I had the honour of addressing High School boys
in their class-room on Bunker's Hill and speaking of fraternity.

union . . ." that is, a union of thirteen States ; the new flag being bright with thirteen stars and thirteen stripes (now forty-eight stars for forty-eight States, with thirteen stripes).

Alas ! it grieves all—Americans and British—to recall that another war took place after Washington's death ; but we will now tell no story of the battles on sea and land ; except this : Fort McHenry, at Baltimore City, in Maryland, was besieged by British ships, which fired shot and shell from the harbour. Francis Key watched in the grey dawn (Sept. 14, 1814), and saw that the fort still held out, and the U.S.A. flag still fluttered above ; and then, on the back of an old letter, he wrote the lines :

" Oh ! say, can you see, by the dawn's early light,
What so proudly we hailed at the twilight's last gleaming ? . . .

CHORUS

" Oh ! say, does that star-spangled banner yet wave
O'er the land of the free and the home of the brave ? "

A White House was built for the President at a new city, named after the General, " Washington," and Washington, not long before his death, walked through its stately chambers. He died at Mount Vernon, 1799. A voice in the U.S. Congress (Parliament) declared that he was " first in war, first in peace, and first in the hearts of his fellow-citizens." Off the shores of England the British fleet lowered its flags to half-mast, when the news of his death was received. Washington left word, in his last will and testament, that, at his wife's death, all slaves on the farm should be freed.

He had given advice to his fellow-citizens of the U.S. Republic not to become " entangled " in the affairs of Europe ; and it was good advice for that time. But the world changes. In 1914, the World War opened, and American citizens were killed at sea by shots from German submarines. The United States, 3,000 miles away, was brought near to Europe by the feeling that unjust conduct must be resisted. In April, 1917, America joined the

Allies. In that same month, Mr. Arthur J. Balfour, a British Statesman, visited Mount Vernon, laid a wreath on Washington's tomb, and made a speech to the people, in which he reminded them that, in his youth, Washington was a British citizen ; and Mr. Balfour added—" There is no place in the world where a speech in the cause of liberty would be better made than here at the tomb of Washington."

LESSON ON WILLIAM WORDSWORTH

The boy William loved to skate on frozen lakes, to fish on the lake in summer time, to go nutting in the woods, to row boats, to climb hills in Cumberland, where he was born (1770). Hot temper he had. Angry with his grandfather for I know not what, William went up into an attic, seized a foil (button-on-end sword used for fencing), and aimed at his breast . . . and dropped the foil ! In quieter moments, he loved to watch sky and earth, storm and seven-coloured bow—

> " My heart leaps up when I behold
> A rainbow in the sky."

He went to school, taught by a dame. If the dame called a register, he answered " Present," to the name of William Wordsworth ; and a little girl answered " Present " to the name of Mary Hutchinson. Other schools he attended, and then, like Milton (whose poetry he loved), became a student at the University, past which " Camus, reverend sire, went footing slow, his mantle hairy, and his bonnet sedge." He too, like Milton, had a fellow-shepherd, named Jones. Wordsworth and Jones set out on a walking tour, staff in hand, without knapsacks, each carrying his " needments " tied up in a pocket-handkerchief, with about £20 apiece in their pockets ; and so, across France and its plains, the Swiss mountains, and by lakes and through the fair cities and villages of blue-skied Italy, the land of Virgil and Saint Francis. Yet often William's thoughts turned to England—Cambridge—the lakes—the waterfalls and stream in Duddon Valley—and his thoughts were thoughts of love :

> " I travelled among unknown men,
>   In lands beyond the sea,
>   Nor, England, did I know till then,
>   What love I bore to thee."

Back to Cambridge and to books ; then walking again amid the grand hills of Wales ; and then he seemed to hear the shouts of the people in Paris, and see the waving of the red-white-and-blue flag of the Revolution, and he must needs go to France (1791-2) and see for himself. In Paris he heard the Republicans sing the " Marseillaise." He saw men borne on the tumbril to the guillotine for beheading. In a high, dark, lonely chamber he lodged, and he could look down upon the streets, and it seemed to him as if Paris could never be at peace again, and he seemed—

> To hear a voice that cried
> To the whole city, " Sleep no more ! "

In the woods, valleys, gardens of England he travelled and dwelt with his sister Dorothy. She used her eyes to watch for him, her ears to listen for him, her hands to help ; she cried if he suffered, she laughed if he rejoiced.

> " She gave me eyes, she gave me ears,
>   And humble cares, and delicate fears,
>   A heart the fountain of sweet tears,
>   And love, and thought, and joy."

And then Mary Hutchinson, who had sat in the dame's school and learned lessons with him, became his wife. She warned him if he approached danger, she comforted him in sorrow and distress, she commanded when she thought his steps went towards things foolish :

> " A perfect woman, nobly planned,
>   To warn, to comfort, and command."

In a pleasant cottage they lived, among the mountains, and near lakes that glistened under sun and moon and stars. Yet he was not idle and at ease. He looked out on the restless world, and, wherever men fought for freedom and better life, his thoughts flew forth to them. Early in the morning, ere it was yet light, he would trudge up the hillside, and along the pass, to meet the messenger who carried journals that told of the War in Spain. Napoleon Bonaparte's armies were slowly retreating across Spain, back to France, before Wellington's soldiers. The hearts of the people of Spain rejoiced as mile after mile of their land was freed from the invader, and the heart of the English poet rejoiced in the peaceful home by the still waters of Grasmere.

Sometimes he would stroll by the waterside, and admire (oh ! great was his *admiration* for things beautiful) the yellow daffodils that grew on the bank, nodding under the wind.

> " When all at once I saw a cloud,
>   A host, of golden daffodils,
>   Beside the lake, beneath the trees,
>   Fluttering and dancing in the breeze."

In after moments, lying on his couch, he often saw the golden dancers with the eyes of imagination.

Once he wrote a letter-poem to his brother James, telling how he talked with the curly-haired little girl who was one of a family of seven ; but a sister and brother had died, and lay buried in green graves in the churchyard. She still said the children were seven, not understanding that two would not return.

> " A simple child, dear brother Jim,
>   That lightly draws its breath,
>   And feels its life in every limb,
>   What should it know of death ? "

He who loved talking with country children loved also to talk with a fellow-poet. At the fine mansion of Abbotsford, by the rippling Tweed, he visited Sir Walter Scott. Sir Walter, very weak in health, listened smiling to a lady who chanted old ballads to the music of her harp. Next year, the poet of the " Lady of the Lake " was dead.

Wordsworth's heart could beat with *hope* for the Spaniards. It beat in sorrow for a Man of Colour in the West Indies—Toussaint. Noble Toussaint was a leader of negroes struggling to be free—a man that had had great power in a West Indian Island, and yet had no desire to hurt the Whites. By Napoleon's order he was seized and taken oversea to France, and placed in a prison on the Jura mountains, near Switzerland, where the cold air killed him. Wordsworth declared the black hero should be remembered in *love*, as indeed you and I remember him to-day :

> " There's not a breathing of the common wind
> That will forget thee."

So admiring, hoping, loving, the poet lived his life ; and he thought a man who did not admire, hope, or love, did not truly live—" We live by admiration, hope, and love."

This beautiful poetic line is from " The Excursion," a story in verse of wanderings over hills and vales, and talks and musings. Such excursions Wordsworth often took ; and passers-by would hardly have taken him for an illustrious poet as he strode along, clad in grey shepherd's-plaid, and shod with heavy hob-nailed boots. Perhaps the country-maid did not think much of poets when she observed Wordsworth and his friend Coleridge trying to take the collar off a horse and failing.

" Ha, masters," she said, " you don't go the right way about the work."

So saying, she turned the collar upside down, and easily drew it off the horse's neck !

The flower he particularly loved was the daisy :

> " Sweet flower ! belike one day to have
> A place upon the poet's grave,
> I welcome thee once more."

At Rydal Mount, his home for many years, Wordsworth

died, 23rd of April (Shakespeare's death-day), 1850 ; and he was buried in the churchyard at Grasmere. Daisies grow on the grave. A daisy may give shade to a dewdrop, and save the lovely gem of water for a while from being dried up by the sun's heat :

> " Small service is true service while it lasts ;
> Of friends, however humble, scorn not one :
> The daisy, by the shadow that it casts,
> Protects the lingering dewdrop from the sun."

The same heart that respected the modest daisy respected a blind child. There may be something great and fine in each of us, seeing or blind : " We feel that we are greater than we know."

When on a visit to Oxford he called at the house of Mr. Gilbert, whose little daughter, Bessie, had been blind since she had fever at the age of three. Bessie could see neither daffodil nor daisy, but she would touch the petals of a flower with reverence, as if she felt the beauty which she could not behold.

She sat alone in a room one day, when Wordsworth entered. He stood awhile silent before the blind girl, as she would often stand before a lovely flower. Her sensitive face looked up, inquiring. Then he gravely said :

" Madam, I hope I do not disturb you."

He could not speak more respectfully to a queen.[1]

At this point, I venture to comment on a problem of some difficulty. An examination of the preceding scheme would reveal that no dominant place has been given to war and to warriors, whether famous leaders or the men of the ranks. It may rightly be inferred that, as an old worker in the cause of International Arbitration and Peace, I should have a strong motive for this attitude. Nevertheless, two things need to be said.

The philosophy of history, as I understand it, cannot

---

[1] Anecdote in Frances Martin's " Elizabeth Gilbert " (1891).

assign to the act of warfare a prime place in human evolution. Civilization is the gradual training of our race in mutual respect and co-operation. This noble process is realized in a variety of developments, economic, social, political, æsthetic, scientific, religious. It is hindered by many forms of exploitation associated with sex, colour, race, money-power, intellectual power, and so on ; and they operate (a fact much overlooked) in times of peace. Hence, in times of peace, the forces of civilization are in perpetual conflict with the exploiting spirit. The main currents of history, indeed, are expressions of these victorious forces. In war, these forces of civilization are still in action, for the worst wars are never mere brute battle ; in the worst wars— I mean the most bloody wars—issues of justice are more or less obscurely recognized and tested. Unless this principle is assented to, much of history is a tragic negation and futile horror, and even the resistance of the Greeks against the Persians at Salamis, or the English against Philip's Armada, or the War of Independence conducted by Washington, becomes an episode of sheer sin. Such a view of human affairs I abhor and reject. So vital and urgent is civilization that, at moments, its progress has to be purchased by war itself. But the essential story of civilization must rank first in our record, and in educational value. The war-instrument is so wasteful of precious life and capacity, that common sense, religion, and the League of Nations should combine to put an end to its ghastly existence—not because there is any intrinsic worth in peace as such, for there is none ; but because the conscience and wisdom of humanity can devise purer and surer methods of vindicating the claims of civilization.

Having spoken with such emphasis on the evil of war, I am the more bold to demand respect and sympathy, and in many cases, reverence for those (a minority of brutish war-mongers excepted) who, through the ages, have given their lives in sacrifice on the altar of civilization. I think, as I write, of my only son, who fell in action near Arras (1917), and who lies in an unknown grave, if his poor shell-torn body could be consigned to a grave at all. I knew his honourable motives in volunteering for the British Army. Why am I not to believe that—relatively to time, place, and social education and ideals—untold millions of other men, both in the World-War of 1914–1918, and in all the wars of all our chequered human past, acted with impulses equally honest and valid? Through all the strifes of human time, most soldiers who fell in any war whatever were mourned by women's tears, as sincere as they were bitter. I speak with deliberation when I say that the spirit of malignity, which works most subtly when it wears an appearance of fraternity and peace, expresses itself very meanly in speaking with contempt of men who risk life or health in the awful field of war.

I conclude, therefore, that the teacher of the young should use every endeavour to enlist the soul of youth in support of international goodwill; but, at every stage of historical study, should treat the men who risked health or life in war as if they were his own suffering kinsmen. This in nowise forbids the allotment of praise or blame to this side or that in a conflict. But it implies respect for sacrifice.

TIME BEFORE MAN *(many millions of years)*.	Nebula, or fire-mist (?). Sun and planets ; starry heavens. Earth, its sponges, corals, shell-fish, sea-weeds ; granite. Fish, insects, reptiles, birds ; moss, trees, flowers ; slate, sandstone, coal, limestone, chalk. Mammals ; monkey-like or ape-like men, 500,000 or more years ago. Ice age.

HISTORY OF HUMANITY

EARLY AGE *to about* A.D. 400	Primitive man ; growth of villages, cities, nations ; slavery. Egypt, Babylon, Assyria, Hittites, Minoans, Persia, Greece, Rome, India, China. Jews and Early Christians. Magic, religion, science, art, literature.
CATHOLIC-FEUDAL AGE *to about* 1300.	Catholic institutions, art, literature. Arabian and Mohammedan religion, art, literature. Moors in Spain. European defence through many centuries against Huns, Mongols, Turks, etc. Crusades. Barons, serfs, manors. Towns and guilds. Rise of modern European nationalities. Parliaments. Chivalry, romances, miracle-plays. School-men, Universities. Trade routes ; use of money extended. Sketches of history of India, China, Japan, etc. Gunpowder.
AGE OF EXPANSION (of learning, science, art, trade, nationality, democracy, and of mankind over the globe) *to the War*, 1914–1918, *and the League of Nations*, 1919.	Printing-press ; spread of learning ; Renaissance. Routes to India and America ; circumnavigation of globe ; trading companies. Protestants, Puritans, and their literature. English revolution, and its literature. Expansion of science. Banks, increased oversea trade ; negro slavery. Beginnings of British Empire-Commonwealth, and of N. and S. American Colonies. Spread of machinery ; Industrial Revolution. Science, art, literature. Rationalists. American and French Revolutions. Australasia colonized. South American Republics. American Civil War. Negro slavery abolished universally. Evolution theories ; Comte, Darwin. Nineteenth-century science, art, literature. Trade Unionists, Co-operators. Suffrage. Popular education. Sanitation, including tropics. German Empire. Italian unity. Rise of Japan. African exploration and Colonies. Socialists. International movements. Union of S. Africa, completing the Home-rule series of Canada, Newfoundland, Australia, New Zealand. Political movement in India. World practically explored and mapped. British Commonwealth renewed in war, and its friendships with U.S., France, Italy, etc., strengthened. Opening of work of League of Nations, including Labour Office. Science, art, literature.

CHAPTER V

THE SCHEME RENEWED FOR ADOLESCENTS

FOR young citizens, aged 14 to 21, our scheme will be renewed in some such Table as is here presented, with the addition of an emphasis on science. I disdain to take account of the fact that modern civilization, so earnestly bent upon increased production from the material soil, is not yet so earnestly bent upon increased production from the marvellous human soul. Here I plan for a young citizenhood which, without any exception, includes lads and girls to the threshold of adulthood. Nor shall I stop to discuss what details shall be cared for by the High School, or the Trade School, or the Half-time School at the Works, or the Professional College, or the Studio, or the Experimental Farm, or the Biological Station, or the University. I have neither eyes nor ears for aught but synthesis. The healthy and unfolding life is one harmonious complex, receiving inspiration from history, and aiming at service of family, country, and humanity. On the ground I here occupy, he is my enemy and obstructor who would allure me towards any other end, or tempt me into debate on administrative machinery.

The main elements of the adolescent complex are the same as for childhood. Perturbations, and spiritual storms, and conversions, and crusades we may be duly prepared for at this stage, but there are no fresh funda-

mentals in the human nature, and education should turn
neither to the right hand nor to the left from the path
already marked.   Let the personality be ever so rich
in powers, and let the development be ever so original
and remarkable, the supreme objective is still service,
and the purpose of education is still to convey the social
message to youth.   The highest genius, more than all
other expressions of humanity, is subject to the law of
duty.   I merely recapitulate, therefore, the chief lines
of training : (1) Physical, including discreet views of
sex-responsibilities, facilitated by biology, shadowed
through the finer elements of literature, and consecrated
by religious appeal.   (2) Moral, giving grace (as just
hinted) to the physical life, fostering the historic sense,
supporting social ideals, finding practical expression in
associated pursuits and amusements, and aiming at
service of Family, Country, Humanity ; (3) Æsthetic,
cultivating love of beauty in the arts, environment, and
personality ; (4) Intellectual, realized in systematic
study of the sciences and conscious development of a
sense of logic, never without deep respect for the simple,
everyday common sense, which is the basis of all valid
philosophy ; (5) Practical, that is, directed to service of
the commonwealth through many-sided industry, and
a citizenship (Civics) which takes intelligent account
of economics and social finance.

Details of a scientific curriculum I do not presume to
set out.[1]   In this sphere, as in all others, education will

---

[1] An excellent treatment of this side of education, for earlier
as well as adolescent years, will be found in the "Report on
Science Teaching in Secondary Schools," published by the
British Association for the Advancement of Science (1917).
It was the work of a Committee which included Sir R. A. Gregory,
Professor H. E. Armstrong, Professor T. P. Nunn, and others.

never die for want of a syllabus. It is the synthetic survey and plan that we most need, and are so apt to miss. And here no man can guide us better than Auguste Comte. " True science," he said, " is essentially composed of laws, not of facts " ; and hence, science, in the strict meaning of the term, cannot be taught to children under the age of about 14, for they lack adequate power to generalize. Again, " the human order depends upon the material order," and that is why some knowledge of astronomy, physics, etc., should (for adolescents and adults) precede a study of social science, or sociology, and of ethics ; and it may be as well to point out how Comte's thought here coincides with Karl Marx's materialistic conception of history. On this principle of the more complex and the more noble order of laws resting on the simpler and more material, Comte arranged the leading sciences in the following educational series : Mathematics (logic), astronomy, physics, chemistry, biology, sociology, ethics.

Broadly speaking, this series indicates the order in which the human mind framed these groups of ideas, beginning with the primitive notions of number and measure, and closing (if one may speak paradoxically) with the eternal quest of the good. Therefore, " no one can be really master of any science unless he studies its special history, which again is bound up, at every step, with the general history of humanity " ; and so biography will always accompany the young citizen's studies in each special science. " Science is a ladder, not a dwelling " ; and, if we ask to what satisfying world the ladder takes us, Comte replies that " the Religion of Humanity has to sanctify science " ; in other words, science is an instrument of service. Therefore, with great respect for those who speak otherwise, I venture to reject entirely the so-called ideal of " truth for truth's sake." I could never offer truth as, in itself, a worthy goal for youth or manhood. To speak in a figure, Satan himself might employ his leisure in such a pursuit, and still be the unmitigated Devil. This is not by any means to say that he who searches for the true laws of nature without, or of the human soul, will perpetually devise practical applications. But it implies a perpetual feeling that the final reference as to value lies in the bearing of knowledge upon human welfare and the glorious unfolding of our racial capacity.

Comte proposed that, each year, from 14 to 21, the young citizenhood of both sexes should hear lectures—" popular lectures," as we should now say— on one of the sciences in the order already named, opening with Logic (mathematics). At first sight, this commencing theme of Logic looks rather forbidding. It may not appear so forbidding if I venture on a few simple hints, thus : Talks on reasoning, illustrated from current discussions on life, manners, industry, politics, drama, etc.; simple explanations of the bearing of calculation, geometry, and mechanics on daily experience and problems ; biographies of eminent mathematicians, and not forgetting such figures as the scholastic St. Thomas Aquinas. In a previous page I have borrowed ideas from the eminent Frenchman, J. H. Fabre, as to methods of lending beauty to mathematics ; and, as to the sciences in general, acquaintance with the writings of Michelet, Ruskin and Maeterlinck—to name only a few examples—should assure any doubter that human genius will not fail to combine exact knowledge with æsthetic. In these days of the illustrated encyclopædia, magic lantern, and kinema, there is very little room left for the sceptic who denies the possibility of interesting the universal crowd in astronomy, physics, chemistry, biology, evolution, hygiene, sex-ennoblement, and sociology. As to ethics, life and history are the standard text-book, and love, imagination, and reason are the interpreters. Two of the culminating interests (rightly understood, indeed, they are *the* culminating interests) of this seven-years' study would be Education, of which all adolescents should be induced to see the profound importance, and human geography, or the effective survey and exploitation of nature for the material service of mankind. Cynics will deride this vision of the masses of humanity feeling an interest in either education or human geography. I am content to remember that the humblest parents who love their children, in a remote Chinese or Indian or English village —however unlettered or however far removed from the academy of calf-leather-binding and robes—do, as a matter of fact, understand the basis of education ; and content also to remember that the humblest barbarians of Central Africa or the Amazons, who procure maintenance from field or forest, do, as a matter of fact, understand the basis of human geography and regional survey. College pedantry is often a greater stumbling block than simple ignorance. Make way for the human soul.

Philosophy recognizes that the sciences are abstract ; that is, they abstract certain facts of experience, and group them under " laws " of mathematics, astronomy, physics, and so on. Hence scientific motives, however

innocent and logical in themselves, ought never to be
the ruling motives.   Life does not divide and abstract ;
it integrates and creates a synthesis.   Therefore, the
arts, which impart a sense of the health, beauty, whole-
ness, and all-embracing genius of life, must rank higher
than the sciences in our final view of education.   By
the arts I here mean poetry, the æsthetics of language
generally (musical prose, elocution, grammatical and
pure speech), music, pageantry, festival, dancing,
drama, painting, architecture, sculpture, gardening,
town-planning, costume, household decoration, the
cultivation of health as a means to personal comeliness,
and that habitual fine behaviour, evolved by goodwill,
which stands as the loftiest achievement of civilization.
But these admirable agents of life must never be left
in the care of the people whom we have hitherto known
as professional artists, professional literary men,
professional masters of ceremonies, and the like.   A
population trained in the love and comprehension of
history necessarily loves and comprehends art.   It
does not take art from lecturers and experts as patients
take doses from physicians.   Its heart, in demanding
beauty, creates its own teachers.   In other words, the
expression of beauty in life arises from a consensus
between the people and the people's interpreters ; or,
if you will, the people and the philosophers.   Hence, in
the adolescent stage of 6 or 7 years, the story of
humanity should be again recited, again studied, in
ampler details, and with fuller discussion of economic,
political, intellectual, and moral issues.   I have pre-
fixed to the present chapter a Table which sufficiently
symbolizes this richer content and wider outlook.   Once
again I plead that literature and art shall not be turned

into detached pursuits,[1] but appreciated in connexion with the age and environment—Primitive, Indian, Persian, Egyptian, Greek, Roman, Catholic, etc., as may happen—which gave birth to their phases of genius and idiosyncrasy. But, all the time, a keen sense of evolution must be maintained ; nor, indeed, can we expect any age of normal human life to feel the charm and impulse[2] of this unfolding process more vividly than the period from puberty to manhood or womanhood ; though, to tell the truth, the joy of it may lend a serene ray to the bed of death itself. And here we discover another reason for adopting the plan of School Celebrations proposed by Dr. Hayward. In such festivals, the skill of composers may gather gems alike from contemporaries and from the succession of the centuries, and so accustom young souls to wide and opulent visions.[3] To souls thus disciplined and enriched the educators of the future will not need to address appeals to study Civics ; nor will statesmen and economists argue desperately on the fundamental value of industry ; nor will prophets beseech a hearing for the message of beauty ; nor will religion seek to reveal the duty of service. We do not ask the lark to sing.

My essential subject all along has been the inspiration of youth. It is assumed that a civilized community will make it a point of honour and of rational economics

---

[1] Except, of course, for technical training, or to satisfy a personal taste ; but, in either case, for a time only ; one should always return to the general and synthetic life.

[2] Bergson's " Élan vital."

[3] One may note, as a happy indication of a finer popular taste, the welcome given to the issue of H. G. Wells's "Outline of History."

alike to ensure that every young citizen[1] is trained for helpful employment, and that not one is left to search painfully for a useful station in the social life. Hence, no "vocational" programme is placed before the reader; nor is any time-table drawn up for continuation-classes, evening lectures, social centres, and the rest. I ask that, both for teachers and adolescent citizens, in every variety of educational institution, and not least in the universities and the technical colleges, the governing thought shall be that we are the children of a great past, co-partners in an order inspired by the history of humanity, and creators of progress. At bottom, there is but one vocation, and all should be enrolled in it. I have frequently used the word Religion. If religion is not a synthesis, that is, if it is not a gathering together and unifying of motives, powers and aims, then it is dead ashes, a worn-out organism, a grinning skull, a threadbare gown that clothes no living herald. There is more real religion in the naïve reverence of Australian blackfellows for their Kangaroo totem—symbol of clan society and mutuality—than in a thousand dry-as-dust (or, perchance, ill-tempered and uncharitable) discussions of the "nature of God" or "truths of Christianity." Alas, that in so many churches the name of God rolls in thunder, and the still, small voice of goodwill to all mankind only bleats or whispers! On the other hand, the bigotry of the Spanish Inquisition was, relatively to the possible wisdom of its age, less guilty towards

---

[1] There should be no need to add the phrase "without distinction of class." Just as a certain type of religion has recited the formula that "every soul is precious in the sight of God," so, to the universal religion here implied, every citizen is a precious social servant.

humanity than the hard theory that despises the long
story of magic, totemism, idolatry, and theology
running through the evolution of man, and would shut
the ears of the world's youth to the poetry, parables,
and legends of the many-sided creeds : Confucian,
Buddhist, Hindu, Hellenic, Roman, Hebrew, Moslem,
Catholic, Unitarian, Mystic.   There are people whose
tongues prate everlastingly of God, and who know
naught of religion except that name.   There are people
who howl at superstition every day, and to whom a
living truth never comes at dawn or sunset.   Between
these two groups of debaters, who oppose each other
in words, but are akin in fundamental quality, I presume,
in humbleness and yet with boldness, to step, and,
as a teacher, to pray for a lasting obliteration of this
line between the sacred and the profane, the religious
and the secular.   Let the disputants retire with their
creeds and their denials.   Leave us and the world's
youth with the complete story of man's admiration,
hope, struggle, suffering, beliefs, illusions, discoveries,
achievements, and love.   Then we can breathe the full
inspiration of the ages.   Then we can build the universal
school.   Make way for the human soul !

In the language of Discussion Circles, I find in such
an attitude " the solution of the religious difficulty "
in British schools.   It implies neither satisfaction
with " State neutrality " to religion nor entrance for
any sectarian or theological " doctrine." It asks for
the grand story, for parables, for poetry, and not for a
thin formula or an article of belief.   And let me say a
word or two as to three countries outside the traditional
British circle of thought and habit ; I mean France,
the United States, and India.   In India I have visited

a selection of vernacular schools and high schools, and I venture to claim a moderate acquaintance with Indian ideas and history.   In America I have seen many schools at work, and I have happily talked, hundreds of times, with classes of American children.   I have no personal knowledge of French schools, but, as regards moral and civic instruction in the Republican institutions, primary and secondary, I possess the salient facts through close examination of text-books and a considerable survey of educational criticism.   My judgment is as follows : The Hindu mind, admirable in its veneration for time-honoured religious philosophy (and I do not forget the so-called " un-educated " peasants), is not equipped with a sense of history as expressed in this essay.   The American mind, as displayed in the splendid grade schools and high schools, is theoretically open to the great experiment I advocate, but, at present, is not adequately conscious of the story of humanity, or of the rich content of the world's many-sided faiths. The French mind, while achieving entire liberation from Roman Catholic limitations, and justly proud of a clear and logical system of ethical and civic instruction,[1] is insufficiently responsive to the imaginative and emotional appeal (I dare not add " romantic," for fear of misunderstanding, but I wish I could), of the thousand years and more of Catholic-feudal piety and culture. In speaking of the American or the French mind, I allude only to its utterance in the public school system. It would be tedious and useless to extend observation to the systems of civilized nations in detail.   One may certainly affirm with truth that no community has adopted the basis which I have tried to describe, and

[1] " La Morale laïque."

which, nevertheless, is the most natural and simple of all. The signs of the educational times, however, tell of our approach towards the adoption of this basis and faith in this inspiration.

When, a few pages back, I used the phrase " universal school," I was thinking of the gradual approximation of methods (they are already approximating) in all the schools of civilization. Let each nation, let each race, retain its spiritual turn of mind, its social art, its teaching polity, so far as to allow of the fruitful expression of the local genius as a contribution to the general human treasury. Consistently with this noble personality in each individual people, all the nations can follow the outline of the scheme I have attempted to portray. Any experienced teacher, touched by the spirit of historical philosophy, could, without serious difficulty, re-shape my two Tables, adapt them to the needs of America, France, India, Brazil, Japan, or any other national instance, and yet leave a recognizable framework and—most important of all—the same definite ideal. Such a method, slowly developed by the educators of the world, will, sooner or later, provide a powerful and magnificent aid in the movement towards universal co-operation and universal religion.

TABLE OF WORLD HISTORY FOR INDIA

TIME BEFORE MAN *(many millions of years).*	Nebula, or fire-mist (?). Sun and planets. Earth, its sponges, corals, shell-fish, sea-weeds ; granite. Fish, insects, reptiles, birds ; moss, trees, flowers ; slate, sandstone, coal, limestone, chalk. Mammals ; monkey-like or ape-like men, 500,000 or more years ago. Ice age.

HISTORY OF HUMANITY

EARLY AGE	Primitive man. Growth of villages, cities, nations. Vedas. Castes. Indian merchants reach Babylon. Buddhists ; influence in Syria, Egypt, etc. Jains. The great epics. Contacts with Greeks, Romans, Persians, Yue-chis, etc. Pilgrims from China.
AGE OF PURANAS AND MOSLEM RULE	Vikramaditya. Rise of Islam in Arabia. Migration of Parsis into India. Rajput and Chola rulers. Great development of Hindu religion, temples, literature. Sankaracharya. Europe, its crusades, printing-press, Parliaments. Akbar and Sivaji.
AGE OF THE MEETING OF EAST AND WEST	European travellers to America and India. Circumnavigation of globe. East India Company. The Sikhs. Beginning and growth of British Empire-Commonwealth. English, American, and French revolutions. Western machinery, Trade Unions, popular education, democracy. Colonies in S. America, Australia, Africa. Suez Canal. Railways, postal service, irrigation, etc., in India. China and Japan influenced by the West. Indian education influenced by the West. Indian Nationalists. Arya Samaj. World practically explored and mapped. Changes under Ripon, Morley, Chelmsford. The World War, 1914–18. League of Nations, 1919

The above Table, adapted to India, may be taken as an example of many possible applications of the scheme of this book to various nationalities.

INDEX

AGRICULTURE, 28-31, 63, 86, 87
Alphabet, 21, 36
Animals, 28, 40, 62
Arch, Joseph, 87
Arithmetic. *See* " Mathematics "
Apocrypha, Jewish, 36
Art, 30, 40, 67, 94, 118, 120
—— and science, 8, 122
Arts, List of, 122
Ashbee, C. R., 95
Augustine, S., 59

BALDI, 98
Baring-Gould, 69, 70
Benedict, S., 69
Bergson, 123
Bible, 3, 7, 27, 36, 39, 40, 67, 84, 95
Branford, B., 19
——, V., 69, 89
Breasted, J. H., 24
Brunhes, 89
Bury, J. B., 50

CALDERON, 95
Calendar, 35, 36
Catholicism, 6, 39, 60, 68, 69, 92, 126
Church, Col., 29
Civics, 38, 42, 85, 86, 118, 123
Civilization, what it is, 113
Cœur, Jacques, 89
Comte, Auguste, 4, 8, 28, 84, 91, 119, 120 ; and Marx, 85, 119
Coomaraswami, A. K., 45
Coulton, G. G., 68
Crete, 30

DANTE, 5, 60, 74, 75
De Candolle, A., 30
Dixon, R. W., 8
Drama, 40, 70, 77, 95
Drawing, 20, 41, 77, 97

EDUCATION, aim, 3, 42 ; social message, 7 ; synthesis, 9, 10 ; order of values in, 3, 23, 85, 118 ; universal, 127
Ænock, C. R., 89
Esperanto, 36, 96

FABRE, J. H., 17
Fairy-tales, 24, 25
Feeling and intellect, 23
Fleure, 64
Folk-lore and Songs, 15, 32, 70, 93
France : education, 125
Frazer, J. G., 31, 51
Froebel, 14

GAMES, 37, 40, 41, 70
Geddes, P., 41, 89, 97
Geography, Human, 89, 121
Geology, 16, 96
Geometry. *See* " Mathematics "
Germain, Sophie, 8, 9
Gilbert, J. H., 87
Gospel, 3
Gregory, Lady, 51
Gregory, R. A., 51, 96
Gretton, R. H., 67
Guest, Lady, 75
Guilds, 37, 58, 62, 65

HALL, A. D., 87
Harris, Rendel, 30
Hayward, F. H., 12, 77, 91, 98, 123
Holdenby, C., 29
Humanity, unity, 8

IMAGINATION, 22, 99
Indian education, 125
Intellect, trained by history, 24

JEUDWINE, J. W., 62, 64, 75, 77
Johnston, H. H., 89

LANGUAGE, 36, 73, 122
Lawes, J. B., 87
Leach, A. F., 73
Leaf, W., 36
League of Nations, 5, 91, 113
Legends, 12, 24, 26, 30, 33, 36, 37, 39, 67, 68, 69, 71, 72, 74, 93, 95, 125
Lessons, Notes of, on India, 43 ; Ireland, 47 ; Rhone, 52 ; Italy, 78 ; Milton, 100 ; Washington, 104 ; Wordsworth, 108
Lenthéric, 56
Literature, 9, 43, 94, 95, 122, 123
Logic and mathematics, 19, 98, 120

MABINOGION, 75
Mahabharata, 33
Maps, 34, 77
Marx, 85, 119
Mathematics, 16, 18, 34, 35, 48, 66, 74, 89, 97, 120
Minerals, 30, 40, 63
Modelling, 41, 63, 77
Mohammed, 72
Money, 31, 60, 66, 89
Montalembert, 69
Montessori, 16
Music, 20, 32, 60, 96

NATIONALITIES, 60
Negativism in education, 61
Noble, Miss M., 45

PARLIAMENTS, 60, 75
Pascal, 4
Pericles, 5
Plants, 16, 29, 40, 62, 86
Pollard, A. W., 70, 95
Protestants, 92
Prometheus myth, 23
Puritans, 92

QUADRIVIUM, 7, 73
Quennell, 77

RAMAYANA, 27, 33, 43, 45
Reading, 21, 42, 97
Relativity in history, 9
Repetitions, Children's, 15
Religion, 11, 12, 67, 95, 124
Religious and secular, 11, 125
Renard, G., 65
Revolution, a secondary conception, 83
Robinson, J. H., 77
Ross, Ronald, 92
Rowley, Charles, 95

SCIENCE and scientific spirit, 19, 20, 39, 96 ; and art, 8, 122
Sciences, Educational order of, 119
Secular and Religious, 11, 125
Serfdom, 59
Sex hygiene, 91
Shaw, W. A., 89
Sharp, C. J., 15, 32, 70
Slavery, 31, 37, 39, 59
Smith, D. E., 36
" Subjects," 7, 9, 10
Synthesis, 9, 117, 122 ; illustrated in lessons, 47, 52, 57, 99

TALMUD, 71
Teachers' liberty, 10, 11, 25, 26
Trivium, 7, 73
" Truth for truth's sake," 120

UNITED STATES education, 125
Universal education, 10, 99, 127
Universities, 73, 117, 124

VIVES, 6

WAR, 27, 31, 37, 112
Watson, Foster, 6, 93
Wells, H. G., 123
Writing, 21, 36, 42, 97

YOUNGHUSBAND, F., 93

Printed in Great Britain by Jarrold & Sons, Ltd., Norwich.